THE
WHISTLEBLOWER'S
DILEMMA

THE
WHISTLEBLOWER'S DILEMMA

SNOWDEN, SILKWOOD AND THEIR QUEST FOR THE TRUTH

RICHARD RASHKE

DELPHINIUM BOOKS
HARRISON, NEW YORK • ENCINO, CALIFORNIA

WHISTLEBLOWER'S DILEMMA
Snowden, Silkwood and their Quest for the Truth

First Edition

Cover and interior design by Jonathan Lippincott

Library of Congress Catalogue-in-Publication Data is available on request.

ISBN 978-1-88-328568-5

15   16   17   18   RRD   10   9   8   7   6   5   4   3   2   1

To
Thomasina

CONTENTS

Preface   ix

Introduction   3
1. The Whistleblower's Dilemma   7
2. Disillusioned: *Edward Snowden*   11
3. Disillusioned: *Karen Silkwood*   27
4. Whom To Tell?: *Snowden*   35
5. Whom To Tell?: *Silkwood*   51
6. Why: *Snowden*   61
7. Why: *Silkwood*   73
8. The Price: *Snowden*   79
9. The Price: *Silkwood*   85
10. Silkwood: *Death*   95
11. Demonization: *Snowden: Publicity Hound, Coward, Liar*   111
12: Demonization: *Snowden: Spy, Traitor, Criminal*   121
13. A Higher Law?   139
14. Demonization: *Silkwood: Heartless Mother, Drug Addict, Mentally Unstable, Plutonium Smuggler, Liar*   145

15. Silkwood: *Asleep at the Wheel* 159
16. Was It Worth It?: *Snowden* 173
17. Was It Worth It?: *Silkwood* 181
Afterword 187

Major Sources and Notes 191

PREFACE

Choosing two subjects to compare and analyze in *The Whis-tleblower's Dilemma* was challenging but offered a broad field of candidates. There was Frank Serpico, the famous New York cop who blew the whistle on the NYPD in the early 1970s. Peter Maas wrote a bestselling book about him and Al Pacino played him in the movie version. There was Dr. Jeffrey Wigand, who blew the whistle on the tobacco industry in the 1990s. Wigand was the subject of a CBS *60 Minutes* story and a movie, *The Insider,* starring Russell Crowe in the title role and once again featuring Al Pacino. There was also the Daniel Ellsberg story. Ellsberg leaked the Pentagon Papers to the *New York Times* in the 1970s and made international headlines. The Justice Department charged him with a felony crime under the statutes of the Espionage Act of 1917. That charge was dismissed by a federal judge because the government had illegally procured evidence against him.

Although Serpico, Wigand, and Ellsberg were important whistleblowers who took on big targets, I ultimately paired

Edward Snowden with Karen Silkwood, a contemporary of Ellsberg.

Karen Silkwood blew the whistle on powerful targets. Like Dr. Wigand, she exposed the wrongdoing of a large and influential company—the Kerr-McGee Corporation and its subsidiary, the Kerr-McGee Nuclear Corporation. Also like Wigand, she pitted herself against an entire industry—the government-protected nuclear industry, vital to the Cold War. And like Snowden, she blew the whistle on the most powerful government agency at the time—the Atomic Energy Commission. In so doing, Karen Silkwood also challenged the CIA, FBI, Oklahoma City Police Department, and Oklahoma State Bureau of Investigation.

Silkwood's death in a car crash in 1974 caused little more than a ripple. But her family's 1979 negligence suit against Kerr-McGee created national headlines. And the superficial but factually accurate movie *Silkwood,* starring Meryl Streep, made Karen Silkwood cocktail party conversation. But the ink has long since dried, the celluloid has faded, and Silkwood's message is largely forgotten.

In analyzing the Silkwood story here, I rely heavily on the research done for my 1981 book, *The Killing of Karen Silkwood*, for the fact-based foundation. I have enhanced that material with new information, and the analysis of her whistleblower dilemma is sharper, broader, and bolder than in my earlier book. I hope that this new information and analysis will lead to a greater appreciation of who Karen Silkwood was and of her important contribution to society, and finally give her the recognition she deserves and a rightful place in a whistleblower hall of fame dominated by men.

The Snowden story is contemporary and ongoing. Just

about everyone who reads the news or watches television or goes online knows who Edward Snowden is—at least superficially. What makes him exceptional is that he went after the National Security Agency (NSA), the most powerful agency in the U.S. government. In so doing, he challenged the Obama White House, the U.S. Congress, the Department of State, the FBI, and the CIA. And he risks going to prison for a very long time, if he isn't assassinated. In analyzing Snowden and his story as a whistleblower, I rely on sometimes contradictory facts found in the work of journalist and author Glenn Greenwald, fellow journalist Luke Harding, author Michael Gurnow, documentary filmmaker Laura Poitras, a comprehensive team-written article published in *Vanity Fair,* and a steady stream of articles published in the British newspaper, the *Guardian*, the *Washington Post*, the *New York Times*, and *The Christian Science Monitor*, between 2013 and 2015.

Discussing Edward Snowden with colleagues, friends, and the strangers I met during walks in the National Arboretum, in pubs, and on the subway in Washington, I learned that everyone who knows who Snowden is has already decided whether he is a traitor or a hero. I also learned that these opinions are, for the most part, based on emotions, false information, or superficial impressions. It is not the intention of this book to try to sway readers in either direction, but to provide a *factual basis* for deciding whether whistleblower Edward Snowden served or betrayed his country.

Although the lives and concerns and circumstances of Edward Snowden and Karen Silkwood are vastly different, they shared the same goal—truth—as they challenged established organizations. Snowden has revealed alleged unconstitutional government programs devoted to collecting electronic bulk data on Americans who were not terrorist suspects. Silkwood blew the whistle on health and safety violations that endangered nuclear workers, their families, and the environment. The issue was life and death.

The Silkwood story has one huge advantage over the Snowden story—distance. Silkwood blew the whistle more than forty years ago. That span of years gives her story a depth and us a perspective that the ongoing Snowden story will one day achieve. Forty years from now, who Edward Snowden was and what he accomplished will be much clearer and arguably less emotional. And its ending will have been written. If what Snowden says is true, and government agents are plotting to kill him, then his end may mirror Silkwood's and dramatically illustrate the whistleblower's dilemma.

Richard Rashke
Washington, D.C.
August 2015

THE
WHISTLEBLOWER'S
DILEMMA

INTRODUCTION

One dry, cold November night in 1974, Karen Gay Silkwood left a union meeting at the Hub Café in rural Crescent, Oklahoma, jumped into her white Honda Civic, and headed down Highway 74 toward Oklahoma City. It was 7:30 p.m., the last day of her life. On the seat next to her were the documents she had stolen from her employer, Kerr-McGee, a contractor that manufactured fuel rods filled with plutonium pellets for the Atomic Energy Commission (AEC). Silkwood planned to deliver the sensitive documents to a *New York Times* reporter waiting at the Holiday Inn Northwest. Her documents included doctored quality-control negatives.

Silkwood may also have had classified or government-protected Kerr-McGee inventory reports showing that forty pounds of plutonium, called "material unaccounted for," or MUF, was missing from the plant. It was an open secret among Silkwood's fellow workers that plutonium was missing. Silkwood discovered the actual size of the shortfall.

A little more than seven miles out of Crescent, Silkwood's Honda Civic crossed over to the left side of the road, straightened out, traveled more than 240 feet down a washboard shoulder, and smashed into the cement wall of a culvert running under the road. She died instantly.

Did Karen Silkwood fall asleep at the wheel as the Oklahoma Highway Patrol ruled, or was she wide-awake when her car sped down the shoulder of the highway, as an independent accident investigator determined? Was it a one-car crash as the state police reported, or did someone force her off the road as the accident investigator concluded?

The answers to these questions still lie buried under layers of secrecy in the files of the FBI, the Justice Department, the Nuclear Regulatory Commission, and the Oklahoma State Bureau of Investigation, which are protected by loopholes in the Freedom of Information Act and Oklahoma's Open Records Act. Those laws allow federal and Oklahoma government officials to exclude from public disclosure—at their own discretion—their secret and possibly embarrassing Silkwood files.

Forty years after Karen Silkwood's death, the questions remain: What are government agencies still hiding? Whom are they protecting?

As troubling as the secrecy issue is after almost two and a half centuries of American democracy, the fundamental questions raised by Karen Silkwood's death and the posthumous 1979 negligence trial against Kerr-McGee, detailed in my book *The Killing of Karen Silkwood,* are much broader. And they are as valid today as they were then. Driven by Cold War fears—both warranted and exaggerated—the United States government and its nuclear contractors sacrificed health, safety, and the environment in order to develop weapons of mass destruction. The Silkwood story asks: *Can government regulators, politicians, the military-intelligence complex, and profit-oriented corporations be trusted to deal responsibly with nuclear energy, hazardous nuclear waste, and the production and management of highly dangerous nuclear weapons? Do they have the will and courage to protect Americans from indifference to life, gross negligence, unaccountable mismanagement, human error, deception, corruption, and greed?*

In his own way, in a different time, and dealing with a different issue, Edward Snowden asked the same questions about the war on terror.

✦

In May 2013, thirty-nine years after the death of Karen Silkwood, computer whiz and uber-hacker Edward Snowden packed up some clothes, a few personal belongings, four laptops, and several thumb drives. Those thumb drives contained thousands of pages of top-secret government documents so well firewalled that even the most accomplished hackers in the world hadn't been able to access them. Snowden then boarded a plane for Hong Kong under his own name, checked into a hotel under his own name, and prepaid his bill by personal credit card.

Like Karen Silkwood, Edward Snowden was about to blow the whistle—not on a major corporation like Kerr-Mc-Gee or a government agency like the AEC, but on the most secret and most powerful intelligence hub in America—the National Security Agency (NSA). Unlike Silkwood, who was on her way to meet *New York Times* reporter David Burnham the night she was killed, Snowden was waiting for reporter Glenn Greenwald to come to him.

David Burnham never had the chance to write an exposé based on Silkwood's documents, which disappeared from her car the night she died. Glenn Greenwald wrote a series of articles that exposed a facet of America's top-secret, electronic snooping program that had been blessed by a top-secret court and secretly approved by the Obama administration. The articles sent tremors around the world.

Like the Karen Silkwood story, the Edward Snowden story raises a string of serious and intriguing questions. Snowden fled to Hong Kong. Was he working for the Chinese, as his critics allege? Next, Snowden took up residence in Moscow. Was he sharing his documents with Russian intelligence officers? Snowden admits copying top-secret NSA documents. Was that theft or was he just returning documents that belonged to the people? Was bulk collection of phone and electronic data on Americans, who were not terrorist suspects, unconstitutional? If so, did the NSA commit a crime if it illegally invaded the privacy of U.S. citizens? Snowden admits that he broke the law when he copied classified files and gave them to the media, but he denies that it was a crime to do so. Did he commit a crime? If he did, was it treason? Snowden says he is willing to face a judge and jury as long as he gets a fair trial. Will the Justice Department guarantee him a fair trial? If Russia eventually decides to expel Snowden, will another country grant him asylum, and if it does, can it protect him from assassins?

In the end, Karen Silkwood paid a heavy price for daring to blow the whistle on Kerr-McGee, the nuclear industry, and the AEC. So might Edward Snowden.

1

THE WHISTLEBLOWER'S DILEMMA

In June 2013, Edward Snowden shoved himself and other whistleblowers like Karen Silkwood into the spotlight when he leaked top-secret National Security Agency (NSA) documents. In so doing, he reminded the nation that whistleblowing is both a First Amendment right, albeit controversial, and a necessity to keep government and commerce honest. Snowden's actions provoked a series of questions ranging from nettlesome to troublesome:

Are whistleblowers heroes or traitors?

Are whistleblowers snitches or saviors?

Do they have a legal, moral, or ethical obligation to blow the whistle?

Do they do more damage than good for the nation?

What personal price do they pay?

Is it worth it?

Most of the hundreds, if not thousands, of whistleblowers never earn ink on the front pages of national newspapers or their online counterparts. Most of the whistleblowers who make headlines do so because they have exposed the secrets of powerful corporations and government agencies with seemingly unlimited resources to hound, scare, silence, and break their critics financially, physically, mentally, and spiritually. Whistleblowers who leak *classified* government secrets force the nation to question the legality or criminality of their controversial activity. These whistleblowers also leave the government with little choice but to charge, try, convict, and sentence them under the Espionage Act of 1917—as the U.S. Department of Justice did with Wiki leaker Chelsea (formerly Bradley) Manning and threatens to do with Edward Snowden, if it can ever extradite him to the United States to face a judge.

✦

A potential whistleblower who discovers wrongdoing is, more often than not, forced to grapple with a life-altering or life-shattering dilemma. What to do?

Look the other way. "It's none of my business."

Rationalize the problem. "It goes on everywhere, so why should I stick my neck out?"

Pass the buck. "It's somebody else's problem, not mine."

Be pragmatic. "Nothing will change anyway."

Protect self and family. "It's too risky."

Get rich. "Doesn't the government pay for information on waste and fraud?"

Blow the whistle. "It's my duty."

Researchers such as sociologists Joyce Rothschild and Terance D. Miethe, who have conducted an extensive survey of whistleblowers and written thoughtful articles on the whistleblowing phenomenon, have provided a context to evaluate and understand both Edward Snowden and Karen Silkwood. One of their important findings is that, unlike Snowden and Silkwood, *at least half* of those who observe wrongdoing in the workplace remain silent. They fear retaliation and believe that blowing the whistle wouldn't do any good. Why take the risk?

Rothschild, Miethe, and other researchers have also discovered striking similarities among whistleblowers who, like Snowden and Silkwood, challenged organizations rather than individuals.

Most or a vast majority of whistleblowers were naïve before they reported wrongdoing. They didn't understand the risks or foresee the consequences. They reported the wrongdoing internally rather than to the media, which they considered a last resort. And they were motivated to blow the whistle by pride in their work and/or by "personally held values."

Most or a vast majority of whistleblowers saw their job performance ratings decline, experienced an increase in the monitoring of their work and phone calls, and were eventually fired or forced to resign. Fellow workers, warned to avoid contact with them, shunned them, making them pariahs in the workplace. Most experienced some form of retaliation by their employer that resulted in severe depression or anxiety, deteriorating physical health, severe financial loss, and stressed family relations. The retaliation against them was greater when the wrongdoing was "systemic"—an essential part of the culture and modus operandi of the organization.

Most or a vast majority of whistleblowers felt that the stress, insecurity, loss of sleep, feelings of isolation and powerlessness, anger, and paranoia damaged their physical, spiritual, and men-

tal health for up to five years. Furthermore, they observed no significant positive change in the organization they blew the whistle on, and they watched the wrongdoer go unpunished.

✦

Of course, whistleblowers can always file a harassment lawsuit against their employer, but the chances of winning are slim. As a complainant, the whistleblower would have to prove that the alleged intimidation and harassment was an unwarranted and deliberate punishment for blowing the whistle. Such cause and effect is difficult to establish in a court of law. Furthermore, the whistleblower would have to fell a Goliath armed with a fat wallet and backed by an army of high-priced attorneys. Already financially stressed, how long could a lone David hold out?

Here lies the whistleblower's dilemma. Given the frightening and predictable consequences, why would whistleblowers like Snowden and Silkwood want to expose illegal activity, corruption, criminal negligence, or fraud?

2

DISILLUSIONED

Edward Snowden

Edward Snowden was a self-taught computer maverick who dropped out of high school at the age of sixteen. Later, professional colleagues called him a genius. He chose to leak his classified NSA documents to Glenn Greenwald, another maverick. Trained as a constitutional lawyer at New York University, Greenwald began his career as a litigation attorney. He went on to become an award-winning author, journalist, and columnist, and an expatriate who worked out of a remote mountain home overlooking Rio de Janeiro.

Greenwald's writings explain why Snowden chose him: his 2001 bestseller, *With Liberty and Justice for Some*, examines the double standard of the U.S. criminal-justice system—one for the powerless and one for high-level government officials. The book made him the darling of privacy-rights activists and the champion of "justice for all." The "all" included President George W. Bush and Vice President Dick Cheney, who approved, according to Greenwald, illegal and unconstitutional invasions of the privacy of American citizens in Trailblazer and StellarWind, NSA's secret bulk-data-collection operations.

"By ordering illegal eavesdropping," Greenwald argued, "the president had committed crimes and should be held accountable for them."

In sum, Glenn Greenwald had a set of sharp teeth and loved to nip at the heels of bureaucrats, politicians, and high government officials. When Edward Snowden first contacted him in December 2012, Greenwald was skeptical. With his international reputation at stake, he was not about to be conned by a self-proclaimed computer professional who said he worked for the U.S. intelligence community. Greenwald approached Snowden with a great deal of caution and a prudent dash of journalistic skepticism. When he finally met Snowden face-to-face seven months after Snowden had first contacted him, Greenwald grilled the former CIA and NSA systems analyst and hacker for five uninterrupted hours. Like a wily prosecutor, he laid traps designed to catch Snowden in lies and inconsistencies, or ducking behind vague answers. After the marathon interview, Greenwald concluded: "Snowden was highly intelligent and rational, and his thought processes methodical. His answers were crisp, clear, and cogent. In virtually every case, they were directly responsive to what I had asked, thoughtful, and deliberate. There were no strange detours or wildly improbable stories of the type that are the hallmark of emotionally unstable people or those suffering from psychological afflictions. His stability and focus instilled confidence. . . . I was convinced beyond any doubt that all of Snowden's claims were authentic and his motives were considered and genuine."

Snowden's subsequent online and media interviews reveal little if anything to contradict Greenwald's observations and conclusions. They show him to be flawlessly articulate. His words flow in an unhurried, gentle manner. Sometimes he's even witty. He never seems to stumble. Or fail to complete a sentence. Or pause in search of the right word. Or sound overly boastful. To the contrary, he projects the image of a calm, confident, and sincere young man with nothing to hide. The only time he appeared nervous was when he first identified himself to the world as Edward Joseph Snowden, the person who had leaked highly classified NSA documents to the media.

For a kid without a high school diploma or GED certificate, Snowden's career path borders on stunning. The following account shows that Snowden was far from the low-level computer geek that government damage controllers tried to make him out to be.

"Ed" Snowden grew up inside the dense Washington-Baltimore corridor, a fifteen-minute drive from the headquarters of the NSA at Fort Meade, Maryland. The National Security Agency—or "No Such Agency" as the NSA is playfully called—occupied an eleven-story steel and glass cube that sits on a 350-acre campus guarded by its own police force and employing more than 30,000 people. Young Snowden was so undistinguished that former classmates and teachers barely remember him. Nor did he stand out as a Boy Scout. If he was remembered at all, it was as a kid obsessed with video games. Later in life he would credit video games with helping to shape his worldview. "The protagonist," he explained, "is often an ordinary person who finds himself faced with grave injustices from powerful forces and has the choice to flee or fight for his beliefs."

Ed Snowden dropped out of high school during his sophomore year, after missing several months of classes due to a bout with mononucleosis and the stress of watching his parents squabble their way into court and a messy divorce. In 1999, after recovering from his illness, he began taking classes at Anne Arundel Community College, a few miles south of Baltimore, to earn a high school diploma. He was sixteen years old.

Because his transcript is incomplete, it isn't clear what courses he took, how many, and when. Two things are quite clear, however. He had no respect for community colleges, and he never received a degree from the college. As he later posted online: "I don't even have a high school diploma." He apparently did earn an advanced certificate as a computer systems engineer.

The young Snowden was gentle, sincere, somewhat reserved, and opinionated. All of his professional life, he was defensive about his lack of academic credentials, not that he had reason to be. His IQ was 140, according to author Michael Gurnow. Politically, Snowden leaned right. (He would later dispute that label, claiming to be a moderate.) A supporter of John McCain for president and a follower of libertarian Ron Paul, Snowden hated government surveillance with a passion, and believed that the Social Security program was a government mistake that encouraged laziness. A gun advocate who owned a Walther P22 that he "loved to death," Snowden opposed President Obama's push to ban assault weapons. On the other hand, he supported a living wage, society's obligation to care for the sick, and women's rights.

As strange as it seems, given what we now know about Edward Snowden, he vehemently opposed the leaking of classified government documents to the media. In 2010, three years before he gave his own cache of highly classified NSA documents to Glenn Greenwald and others, he demonized in an *Ars Technica* online blog the unnamed whistleblower(s) who had leaked to the *New York Times* a secret report about an Israeli plan to attack Iran.

"Who the fuck are the anonymous sources?" Snowden asked during an online chat about the *Times* story. "Those people should be shot in the balls. . . . Are they trying to start a war? . . . That shit is classified for a reason."

Snowden's best friend was his computer, which he believed was mankind's greatest invention. He immersed himself in the world of the Internet, where college degrees and academic credits were irrelevant, and where it was easy to hide behind code names. He soon became a prolific blogger (800 comments) and online chat-buddy with fellow webheads on the *Ars Technica* website under the name The TrueHOOHA. The Internet gave him the chance to say anonymously whatever was on his mind—girls, gaming, the stock market, Japan, sex, the joys of gun ownership. He could be funny, outrageous, and fuck-you opinionated. He posted silly photos of himself: mooning the camera in black underwear; dancing in a tux; sitting in a car in a leather jacket with a photo caption that read: "So Sexxxy It Hurts! Ed Snowden, Gold Plated."

But young Ed Snowden was more than a smart-aleck, fun-loving, Internet hell-raiser. He was a serious student determined to master the computer, and he worked at it tirelessly. "I was interested in figuring out how complex systems fit together," he told *Vanity Fair*, "so I put them together and tore them apart. All day, all night." He kept fit with kung fu exercises.

Until 9/11.

After the attack on the World Trade Center and the Pentagon and the thwarted crash in Pennsylvania, Snowden, an unabashed patriot born into a military family (his father served in the Coast Guard for three decades as a warrant officer before becoming a civil servant), decided to enlist in the U.S. Army as a Special Forces recruit. As he put it: "I wanted to fight in the Iraq war because I felt like I had an obligation as a human being to help free people from oppression." Critics and detractors would later suggest a different interpretation. His so-called altruism, they would argue, was little more than the self-serving defense of a criminal and traitor or the desperate attempt of an unemployed young man in search of security and a paying job.

Boasting of some degree of skill in kung fu, he hoped to become a Green Beret—one of those "Fighting soldiers from the sky, fearless men who jump and die." Given his slight build, spindly legs, and serious nearsightedness, his plan was about as practical as that of a skinny, five-foot-tall basketball player hoping to make the NBA. "My visual acuity ends at about four inches from my eyes," he wrote in a blog. "My optometrist always has a good laugh at me."

In May 2004, the Army sent Snowden to Fort Benning, Georgia, for basic training. He was assigned to the 198th Infantry Brigade's 18-X program designed to fast-track recruits into the Green Berets. First, a candidate had to pass a mental aptitude test, then endure fourteen weeks of rigorous basic training followed by dangerous airborne skill training, after which the recruit received his final yes-or-no evaluation. The chosen few got a Green Beret.

Whether Snowden's Green Beret ambition was realistic or not became moot when, he has claimed, he broke both legs during airborne training—probably a parachuting exercise—in July or August and was honorably discharged in September 2004, four months after he joined the Army.

Snowden's public military record reveals that he did indeed train at Fort Benning and was honorably discharged. The record provides enlistment and discharge dates, but medical information would be in Snowden's private record, available to government agencies like the NSA but not to the public. The fact that government damage controllers have not publicly challenged the broken legs supports Snowden's version of events.

However brief, Snowden's military service informed him about more than just how to assemble an assault rifle and parachute from a training tower. The gung-ho, sand-rat attitude of his fellow inductees and instructors disillusioned him about Bush's war, which, he concluded, had more to do with taking lives than saving them. As he would later say online: "Most of the people training us seemed pumped up about killing Arabs."

Following in the footsteps of his libertarian father, Snowden chose to work for the federal government. Once again, he had a plan that seemed youthfully romantic. Relying on his technical skills, he would work his way up in the U.S. government from a low-level security clearance to a top-level one where, he believed, he could best serve his country with his computer skills. Searching for abuse of power and blowing the whistle, he later said, were not part of his career plan.

Snowden's goal wasn't as naïve as some critics would have

it. The NSA had its roots in World War II, when it was formed as a decryption organization whose goal was to break German and Japanese codes. The agency went on to play a vital—and nearly invisible—role in the Cold War. After 9/11, the U.S. intelligence complex (including the NSA) quickly expanded. The government was so desperate for skilled technicians that it waived traditional academic computer-science credentials, leaving the door wide open for computer whiz kids without degrees. It hired more than 1,900 outside consulting firms, like the Dell Corporation and Booz Allen Hamilton, a management consulting company, to provide intelligence-gathering support at every level—from janitors, security guards, analysts, and field spies to skilled computer techies like Edward Snowden. According to the *Washington Post*, one in four intelligence workers was a contractor, and 70 percent or more of the intelligence community's secret budget went to non-government consulting firms.

It seems that Snowden's first government job, in 2005, at the age of twenty-two, was as a security guard for the Center for Advanced Study of Language (CASL). Embedded at the University of Maryland in a secure building, the Center was a Defense Department–funded language training facility and recruiting ground for the U.S. intelligence community. The largest language research institute in America, it was operated by the NSA, whose headquarters at Fort Meade was just down the highway from the university. Before long, CASL promoted Snowden to computer security specialist, a job that allowed him to tiptoe into the world of intelligence. Within a year, he was working full-time for the CIA as a junior computer and technical expert, a position that came with a high-level security clearance.

"It was tough to *break in,*" he explained in an *Ars Technica* blog, "but once you land a *real* position, you're made. . . . I make $70,000. I just had to turn down offers for $83K and $180K . . . they're going in different directions than where I'm heading. And my coworkers have BSs, MSs, and ten-to-fifteen years of experience. Employers fight over me. And I'm 22."

Nine months after he began working for the CIA, Snowden learned that the agency was seeking skilled technicians willing to work overseas. He applied for a post abroad and ended up in Geneva—a spy hub—under corporate cover (secret identity) and with diplomatic credentials. At the age of twenty-four, he not only had top-security clearance but his computer skills had earned him a coveted post in the heart of Europe, rather than an airless office in a mosquito-coast CIA station. He lived in a four-bedroom, government-issued apartment a few blocks from Lake Geneva with a view of the Rhône, commanded a more than respectable salary, and enjoyed a string of perks. He bought a new, dark blue BMW, drove at breakneck speeds, raced motorbikes, traveled around to places like Bosnia, Romania, and Spain. And he changed his clumsy *Ars Technica* game-name to the playful Wolfking Awesomefox.

Snowden's official CIA title was telecommunications information officer, which translates as "cyber cop and problem solver." His job was critical—to protect the computer networks of the CIA and the U.S. diplomatic community in Switzerland from foreign hackers. Geneva became Snowden's watershed.

From his high-level security perch inside the walled and gated U.S. mission in downtown Geneva, Snowden discovered what he considered to be the unconstitutional bending of privacy laws as well as the day-to-day unethical behavior of the CIA, its station managers, and their field operatives. "Much of what I saw in Geneva really disillusioned me about how my government functions and what its impact is in the world," Snowden later told the *Guardian*. "I realized I was part of something that was doing far more harm than good." It also became apparent to him that President Obama was not only welshing on his 2008 campaign promise to correct the intelligence-gathering abuses of the Bush administration, but was secretly authorizing the NSA to bulk-collect the phone and e-mail messages of Americans.

Disappointed and troubled, Snowden suffered a "crisis of conscience," and he gave serious thought to blowing the whistle then and there. But he decided not to. He wanted to give President Obama one more chance. Furthermore, if he leaked CIA secrets and exposed the agency's unethical operations, he reasoned, he might place CIA field agents in harm's way. He didn't want to take that risk. "When you leak the CIA's secrets," he would later explain, "you harm people. I wasn't willing to do that. But when you leak NSA's secrets, you only harm abusive systems. I was much more comfortable with that."

Unable to continuing working for the CIA as a matter of conscience, Snowden quit in 2009 and joined the ranks of the unemployed.

◆

Back in Maryland, Snowden's online *Ars Technica* comments became angrier, more cynical, and bitter. Wary of working directly for the U.S. government, he took a computer technician job in the private sector with the Dell Corporation, a major NSA contractor, working on sensitive and highly classified intelligence programs. Dell gave Snowden top-level security clearance.

The company posted him to Yokota Air Base outside Tokyo, a welcome change. He had privately studied Japanese for a year and a half, loved Japanese culture, and was an avid fan of Japanese anime. As an NSA cyber-operative in the cyber-warfare program, he had several jobs in Japan, all of which required his high-level security clearance. One was to teach top-level military intelligence officers how to prevent Chinese hackers from compromising their networks. Another more critical task was to create a hacker-proof data backup system—a cybershield—to protect NSA locations around the world. To do that, Snowden had to examine NSA data-collection operations.

If Switzerland had been his watershed, Japan was his turning point.

"I could watch drones in real time as they surveilled the people they might kill," Snowden later told Greenwald. "You could watch entire villages and see what everyone was doing. I watched NSA tracking people's Internet activities *while they typed*. . . . I became aware of just how invasive U.S. surveillance capabilities had become. . . . The more time I spent at NSA in Japan, the more I knew that I couldn't keep it all to myself. I felt it would be wrong to, in effect, help conceal all of this from the public."

✦

In 2012, Dell sent Snowden to Hawaii to work at NSA's Kunia Regional Operations Center at Wheeler Army Airfield, ten miles from Honolulu and Pearl Harbor. The center was hidden behind a ten-foot-high fence topped with barbed wire. Its only sign read, "No Trespassing / Government Property." The facility was known as the Tunnel because it was underground.

Snowden's girlfriend Lindsay Mills, whom he had met in Japan, followed him to Hawaii. Mills was an amateur photographer and dancer with some training in ballet. An exuberant free spirit with blue eyes and long, dark-blonde hair, she wrote a regular blog called "Adventures of a World-travelling, Pole-dancing Hero." On it, she posted self-portraits, some a bit risqué. After her arrival in Hawaii she began doing street performances and acrobatic dancing with Paula and the Pole Kats at the Mercury, a thirtysomethings bar in Honolulu, and joined the Waikiki Acrobatic Troupe. Surrounded by spies, she lived with "E"—as she called Snowden in her blogs—"in a world where people moved like ravens." (Mills can be seen in action on YouTube.)

The NSA Regional Operations Center where Snowden worked was one of thirteen NSA hubs outside of Fort Meade that specialized in cyberspying on China and North Korea. It also tracked terrorist operations in the Philippines, Pakistan, and Thailand. Snowden's job as a high-level systems administrator gave him extensive access to a wealth of secret material that showed the scope of NSA's spying on Americans. "Almost nobody knew it was happening," Snowden later told Greenwald. "I really started seeing how easy it is to divorce power from accountability, and how the higher the levels of power, the less oversight and accountability there was. . . . The state—especially NSA—was working hand in hand with the private tech industry to get full access to people's communication."

With a growing awareness of NSA wrongdoing eating at him like moral acid, Edward Snowden became a whistleblower-in-waiting. All he needed was to complete his understanding of what the NSA was doing and how it was doing it. To do that, he needed to see the agency's raw surveillance repositories. With this goal in mind, he turned down a job offer to become an NSA government employee because, he explained later, the security clearance NSA offered him would not have allowed the file access he needed. Instead, in the spring of 2012 he took a job at Booz Allen Hamilton (BAH) and moved out of the "Tunnel" into BAH's thirtieth-floor office in the Makai Tower in downtown Honolulu.

Employing 25,000 workers and with an annual income of $1.3 billion in intelligence work alone (23 percent of the company's total income), BAH was one of the biggest defense contractors in the country. It held a multimillion-dollar contract with NSA's Threat Operations Regional Center. As a BAH-paid infrastructure analyst (basically, a professional hacker) working for the NSA under BAH's contract with the NSA, Snowden's salary was $200,000 a year plus benefits, including a housing allowance. His primary job was to find and fix the flaws and vulnerabilities in the agency's communications system in order to prevent other countries, especially China, from hacking into it. His additional job was to find exploitable weaknesses in the telephone and Internet networks of countries hostile to the United States that NSA could exploit, which gave him almost unlimited access to NSA computers around the world. A special assignment was to copy millions of NSA mainland files into the Regional Center server. The NSA needed a safe backup in case of a power outage on the mainland or a crippling cyberattack.

Snowden soon developed a reputation at BAH as a non-conformist who wore a hoodie around the posh office and kept a copy of the U.S. Constitution on his desk. His NSA assignments came with the agency's highest clearance, allowing him entrée to NSA's inner snoop-sanctum, where its raw-surveillance data was stored. Once there, Snowden discovered how the NSA was monitoring *the entire* U.S. tele-communications system, and how it was working closely with British intelligence. Most important, his clearance was so special that he could enter and leave NSA's inner sanctum without leaving an electronic footprint. That "ghost user" privilege is one reason why the NSA is finding it difficult to know exactly which files Snowden downloaded.

"I realized they were building a system whose goal was the elimination of all privacy, globally," Snowden said later. "To make it so that no one could communicate electronically without the NSA being able to collect, store, and analyze the communication."

The last straw fell into place.

✦

By 2012, Snowden had become so disillusioned with the president that he could no longer give him the benefit of the doubt. He concluded that the president was *never* going to slow down or derail the runaway train of illegal snooping.

"[Obama] closed the door on investigating systematic violations of law," Snowden explained in a 2013 online chat.

"He deepened and expanded several abusive programs, and refused to spend the political capital to end the kind of human rights violations like we see in Guantanamo, where men still sit without charge."

It was time to blow the whistle.

In the summer of 2012, late at night, in a still office, Edward Snowden began downloading onto thumb drives top-secret, classified documents. In May 2013, he told his BAH bosses that he was ill and needed to take a few weeks of medical leave. He recently had suffered a series of seizures that were diagnosed as epileptic. He may have inherited the disease from his mother, who had epilepsy. Then he quietly slipped out of Hawaii with copies of thousands of NSA top-secret files. He left without warning Lindsay Mills or telling her where he was going, in order to protect her from government harassment. As the world now knows, the theft of these documents became the most serious intelligence breach in U.S. history.

3

DISILLUSIONED

Karen Silkwood

By background and education, Karen Silkwood was an unlikely whistleblower. Like Snowden's father, Karen's dad was
also a World War II veteran. He had served as an Army Air
Corps transport pilot and bombardier, with fifty missions to
his credit. Unlike Lon Snowden, however, Bill Silkwood was
not a career military officer or a postwar civil servant. After
the Air Corps decommissioned him, he returned home to
Texas, where he sold insurance, worked as a contract house
painter, and, with his wife, Merle, raised three daughters.

Born in 1946, Karen grew up in a pre-computer, religious household. She showed little interest in politics. She
wasn't active in the civil rights movement or anti-Vietnam
War protests. And yet she exhibited the personal traits of a
future whistleblower. She was an independent thinker, loyal
to a fault, and tenacious. She wasn't afraid to take risks and
speak out—she even corrected her teachers. She put everything she had into whatever she took on.

Unlike Snowden, Silkwood socialized with ease, laughed

a lot, and loved a good time. She played flute in her high school band and was the server on the girls' volleyball team. After school hours, she volunteered at a hospital and belonged to Future Homemakers of America.

Like Snowden, Silkwood was smart. She was a straight-A student, a member of the National Honor Society, and one of twenty-two honors graduates in her high school class of 1964. She studied hard and read a lot. Chemistry was her favorite high school subject, and she was the only girl in her advanced chemistry class. She passed the course with honors and was elected president of the science club. After graduation, she matriculated at Lamar College in Beaumont, Texas, on a one-year scholarship awarded by the local Business and Professional Women's Club. She majored in medical technology.

✦

Love altered Silkwood's career path. The summer after she graduated from high school, she met Bill Meadows. Karen and Bill, who lived in Los Angeles, were vacationing on their respective grandparents' farms near Longview, Texas. They dated over the summer. Bill returned to Texas the following summer to work for the Mobile Pipeline Company. He and Karen eloped because Karen's father opposed the marriage. She was only nineteen years old, a promising student with a future in medical technology. Bill Silkwood was convinced that a marriage would destroy her future. He was right.

Karen dropped out of Lamar College and became a gypsy-wife, migrating with her husband from town to town across Texas—Longview, Corsicana, Sweetwater, Midland,

Seminole. They finally ended up in Duncan, Oklahoma, bankrupt, with three children and a marriage that was falling apart. Karen's father, bitterly against the marriage, was so disappointed in his daughter that their relationship remained strained for the rest of her tragic life.

Bill Meadows offered Karen an uncontested divorce if she would agree to give him custody of their children, Beverly (Kristi), Michael, and Dawn. She refused. Finally, in 1972, after seven years of marriage, she tossed in the towel and walked out of the house without explanation, leaving her children in the care of their babysitter, whom Bill would later marry. Two days later, Karen called Bill from Oklahoma City and told him that she would agree to an uncontested divorce and grant him custody of the children if he granted her visiting rights. And she took her name back—Karen Gay Silkwood.

✦

Silkwood was a low-level clerical worker at an Oklahoma City hospital when she heard that the Kerr-McGee Corporation was hiring laboratory analysts at its plutonium plant on the Cimarron River, near Crescent. Like Snowden's employers—the Dell Corporation and BAH—Kerr-McGee was a U.S. government contractor. Both Dell and BAH worked for the CIA and the NSA; their job was to help the United States win the war on terror. Kerr-McGee worked for the Atomic Energy Commission (AEC). Its job was to provide enough high-grade uranium and plutonium to build a Cold War nuclear arsenal to protect the country from the Soviet Union.

To Karen Silkwood, working in a Kerr–McGee laboratory seemed a heaven-sent opportunity to use her technical talents, build a career, and make more money. So in August 1972—eleven years before Ed Snowden was born—Silkwood donned a white laboratory smock and began to work in the Kerr–McGee Metallography Laboratory. The lab inspected plutonium pellets that workers had shaped into what looked like gray bullets. One inch long and a half inch wide, the pellets were composed of seven parts uranium and three parts plutonium. They were highly radioactive.

The AEC had given Kerr–McGee classified specifications for its pellets. If they were too small, assembly-line workers rejected them. If too large, they skinned them down to size with their hands inside sealed gloves that were inserted in sealed boxes. As a final check, workers examined each pellet to see if it was cracked or chipped. Then they loaded the pellets that had passed initial inspection into fragile, eight-foot-long, pencil-thin stainless steel rods. Next, they washed the tips of the rods with alcohol to remove all radioactive contamination, taking care not to kink the rods. Workers then wheeled the rods into a huge X-ray room where electronic eyes read the contents of each rod. It was a critical step in the final check.

Like Snowden, Silkwood held a job that was both important and responsible. She did a series of quality-control checks in the Metallography Laboratory. She randomly selected pellets from a lot, then held them against an unexposed X-ray film to test for gamma rays. The AEC required that the plutonium be evenly distributed throughout the pellet. If it wasn't, the developed film would show "hot spots" and Silkwood would reject them as dangerous.

Silkwood also polished randomly selected fuel-rod welds to see if there were any cracks or inclusions. If the pellets or welds flunked, she would run tests on the entire pellet lot. If she found a pattern of flaws, she'd reject the lot, which slowed down production and cut into Kerr-McGee profits.

✦

In November, three months after Silkwood began polishing plutonium rod welds, she was pacing outside Kerr-McGee's chain link fence carrying her first ON STRIKE placard. The company's workers were demanding better training, improved health and safety programs, and higher wages.

Silkwood was no union activist. In fact, she had shown little interest in the Oil, Chemical and Atomic Workers Union (OCAW), which represented 150 Kerr-McGee rank and filers. She had joined the OCAW because she saw it as the workers' only protection against one of the largest energy conglomerates in the United States. It was her *duty* to picket, and Karen Silkwood took her turn.

The strike dragged on for ten weeks, and the OCAW local 5-283 came out barely breathing. The Kerr-McGee Nuclear Corporation—a subsidiary of the Kerr-McGee energy empire—wasn't hurting in the fall of 1972, so it could hold out against the strike. And because the winter of 1972–73 was exceptionally cold, jobs were scarcer than usual. Farms for miles around Crescent were filled with unemployed twenty-year-olds, and Kerr-McGee had no trouble cherry-picking strikebreakers to keep its pellets moving. Three dollars an hour ($17 today) seemed like a lot of money to them.

It was an unspectacular strike. No violence, just a war of

attrition. As it stretched into its second month, with Christmas looming, more and more union members abandoned their strike placards and crossed the line, until only a score were left still pacing. Silkwood was one of them.

Two months after the strike began, Karen Silkwood was back at work under a new, two-year contract written by Kerr-McGee. For the twenty OCAW members still left in the battered local, it had been a total defeat. There would be no better training, no improved health and safety measures, and wages remained static. But for Karen Silkwood, the strike had been an awakening. Taking a stand against Kerr-McGee, walking the line, living off part-time wages as a clerk in a building supply company, watching OCAW members knuckle under to pressure one by one—all of these experiences cemented Silkwood's ties with the union and changed the nature of her relationship with Kerr-McGee.

✦

In the spring of 1974, a year and a half after the strike had ended and under pressure from the AEC, Kerr-McGee speeded up production. There were twelve-hour shifts, seven-day work weeks, and uninterrupted rotation from day to night shifts. Speed, fatigue, and corner-cutting caused spills, contaminations, and more spills. Face respirators designed to filter out airborne plutonium particles were defective, worker turnover was high, and more and more untrained workers were handling radioactive metals.

Silkwood worried increasingly about health and safety, about nineteen-year-old farm boys with tractor grease under their fingernails treating plutonium like fertilizer, and about a management that used them up and sent them back to plow the fields with plutonium in their bodies. They had no idea they were *hot*.

But then, on July 31, 1974, a year and a half after the strike ended, Silkwood's concern about health and safety became personal and frightening. She was working alone in the Emissions Spec Lab that day with her hands inside a sealed glove box. Her task was to pulverize plutonium pellets, then examine the dust through a spectrograph to make sure the pellets were not overly polluted with other metals such as nickel and chromium. If they were, she rejected them. After she left the lab, technicians made a routine check on the air-sample filter papers used in the lab radiation monitor while Silkwood was working there. They were "hot." Silkwood had been breathing radioactive air during her shift.

Following company protocol, a health physics technician took nose and mouth swabs. They were positive. Then the tech ordered Silkwood to take a shower, scrub with a wire brush, and provide urine and fecal samples for testing by an outside company. A few days later, the results came back—positive. But not to worry, the head of the health physics department assured her in a private conference; her contamination was insignificant by AEC standards.

When union elections rolled around the week after her contamination in the Emission Spec Lab, Silkwood was mad—and ready. Negotiations for a new two-year contract with Kerr-McGee would begin in three months, and health and safety were at the top of the union's list of demands. Silkwood didn't campaign for a spot on the three-person OCAW bargaining committee. But she was so disillusioned about the ballyhooed commitment of Kerr-McGee and the

AEC to the health and safety of their workers that she let it be known she wouldn't turn the position down if elected. She won—the first female committee member in Kerr-McGee history. Her assignment was health and safety. Jack Tice, who chaired the union's bargaining committee, asked Silkwood to keep her eyes open and to take notes. He had a plan.

For the rest of August 1974 and well into September, Silkwood tracked contamination accidents, questioned health physics technicians, interviewed workers during coffee and lunch breaks, and scoured the plant for safety violations. She wrote her dated observations neatly in a small spiral notebook. She made no attempt to hide from Kerr-McGee management what she was doing. Plant managers had to be blind not to notice.

By late September, armed with a notebook filled with duly dated descriptions of contamination and health and safety violations at the Kerr-McGee Cimarron plant, Karen Silkwood was ready and eager to blow the whistle.

4

WHOM TO TELL
Snowden

Edward Snowden first reported his ethical concerns to his superiors and colleagues over a period of six months. He even showed them evidence of alleged unconstitutional wrongdoing. And he deliberately chose not to blow the whistle to Congress because he viewed it as part of the problem.

"Those efforts were almost always rebuffed," Snowden complained to Greenwald. "They would say this isn't your job. Or you'd be told you don't have enough information to make those kinds of judgments. You'd basically be told—not to worry."

Snowden was more specific about his inside whistleblowing attempts in a 2014 interview with the *Washington Post*. He told reporters that while he was working for the National Security Agency as a Booz Allen Hamilton employee in Hawaii he had voiced his ethical and moral concerns to four superiors—two in NSA's Technology Directorate and two in the agency's Threat Operations Center, where he worked. In the *Post* interview, Snowden said he not only told the four superiors that he was concerned about the volume of data the NSA was collecting about unwitting Americans but he also showed them a color-coded NSA heat map that continuously tracked NSA electronic data collection on Americans . . . *in real time.*

After allegedly blowing the whistle to deaf ears for months, Snowden decided he had no choice but to go public. His logical leak targets were the *Washington Post* and the *New York Times,* two newspapers that commanded domestic and international respect and had a history of welcoming whistleblowers. The problem was that Snowden didn't completely trust either newspaper. In his mind, they were not aggressive enough and were overly cautious in dealing with government wrongdoing.

In spite of his misgivings, however, Snowden eventually gave the *Washington Post* a set of classified documents describing PRISM, a top-secret NSA surveillance program (chapter 6 includes a description of PRISM). Snowden gave the paper seventy-two hours to publish a PRISM story, or he would offer his documents to another newspaper. His skepticism and mistrust of the *Washington Post* turned out to be well founded. After reviewing the PRISM files, the *Post* assembled a team of lawyers to consider the legal implications of publishing a story about the highly classified snooping program and to advise the paper about the legal risks of doing so.

According to Snowden, the attorneys made unreasonable demands, while issuing bone-chilling liability warnings to *Post* management. In the end, Snowden concluded that the newspaper—though not necessarily its reporters—was paralyzed by fear. As Greenwald put it in his book *No Place to Hide*, Snowden was "livid that the *Post* had involved so many people, afraid that these discussions might jeopardize his security."

✦

Like Snowden, Glenn Greenwald didn't trust the *New York Times* or the *Washington Post*. Greenwald saved his most vicious attack for the *Post*, which he thought embodied "all the worst attributes of U.S. political media: excessive closeness to the government, reverence for the institutions of the national security state, routine exclusion of dissenting voices." According to Greenwald, the *Post* allowed the government "to control disclosures and minimize, even neuter their impact"; the *Post* editors would actually approach government officials and advise them about what they intended to publish. National security officials would then tell the editors "all the ways in which national security will be supposedly damaged by the disclosures." Then both sides would begin time-consuming negotiations on the language and extent of the disclosures.

Although Greenwald respected some *Post* reporters like Pulitzer Prize–winner Barton Gellman (who no longer worked at the paper full time), he was highly critical of what he considered the newspaper's political bias. "The *Post* editorial page," he wrote, "remained one of the most vociferous and mindless cheerleaders for U.S. militarism, secrecy, and surveillance." The *Times* wasn't much better. The paper, he charged, had blocked the publication of articles about NSA eavesdropping for more than a year for political reasons.

Snowden e-mailed Greenwald in early December 2012,

using the code name *Cincinnatus*. The moniker signaled how Snowden viewed himself: Cincinnatus was a Roman soldier-hero who relinquished the sword for the plowshare only to be appointed military dictator when Rome was threatened. After defeating the empire's enemies, the Roman Cincinnatus did the unthinkable. He voluntarily gave up political power and returned to the plow.

Cincinnatus's first message to Greenwald was vague. He simply said: "The security of people's communication is very important to me" and went on to say that he had some "stuff" that might interest Greenwald. He declined to discuss what that stuff was without privacy protection, insisting that Greenwald install PGP (Pretty Good Privacy) encryption software before he would say any more online. The software would allow only authorized persons to read e-mails and stop snoopers and hackers at the gate. PGP encryption codes are so complex that Snowden offered to help Greenwald install the software.

Cincinnatus's demand was reasonable. In fact, Greenwald already had PGP encryption on his to-do list, but it wasn't close to the top. Cincinnatus's opening gambit was so ho-hum that Greenwald was hardly intrigued enough to press for more detail. Like most successful journalists and authors, he got more than his share of unsolicited e-mails and letters promising big scoops. The sources rarely delivered. Besides, who *was* this Cincinnatus? Was he or she for real? Or just another web wacko? Why should Greenwald waste his time playing computer footsy with what could be an Internet ghost?

Although Greenwald ignored Cincinnatus, he couldn't dismiss him. Over the next seven weeks, his reporter voice kept whispering, what if this is the big one? Eventually, he e-mailed Cincinnatus and promised to have PGP installed over the next couple of days. But then he didn't. The brushoff frustrated Cincinnatus, who had been expecting a show of enthusiasm. "Here I am ready to risk my liberty, perhaps even my life, to hand this guy thousands of top-secret documents from the nation's most secret agency," Snowden recalled. "And he can't even be bothered to install an encryption program."

If it had not been for his colleague and friend Laura Poitras, Glenn Greenwald would have been guilty of—in his own words—"blowing off one of the largest and most consequential national security leaks in U.S. history."

✦

Poitras was an award-winning documentary filmmaker who specialized in exposing government lies, hypocrisy, and misdeeds. Like Greenwald, she had an international follow- ing and was both a privacy advocate and an expatriate. Her strong views had earned her a place on the U.S. "watch list." Homeland Security agents in New York and at international borders had repeatedly seized her laptops, mobile phones, cameras, and notebooks and had threatened and quizzed her—whom did she meet? where? when?—so many times, whenever she returned to the U.S. after a filming safari, that she chose to live temporarily in Berlin. Her controversial 2006 film, *My Country, My Country,* about the lives of Iraqis under occupation, had been nominated for an Academy Award and sealed her reputation as "a notable thorn in the side of the U.S. military." Her second film, *Oath,* took on Bush, Cheney, habeas corpus, and Guantanamo Bay. Poitras was working on a third film about pervasive domestic surveillance when Snowden approached her.

Snowden had read about Poitras's abusive treatment at the hands of intelligence officials in one of Greenwald's *Salon.com* columns. He had also admired her eight-minute interview with former NSA cryptographer and technical director William Binney, a whistleblower who had reported his concerns about the Bush administration's illegal spying on Americans to Congress, the Department of Defense, and the Supreme Court before he went public. (The Poitras/ Binney interview can be seen on YouTube.)

At the end of January 2013, two months after Greenwald brushed him off, Snowden e-mailed Poitras under the code name *Citizenfour.* "I am a senior member of the intelligence community," Snowden began. (Actually, by rank, he was a junior member of the intelligence community doing the work of a senior member.) "This won't be a waste of your time," he told the filmmaker.

Poitras was skeptical at first. Could the writer of the e-mail be a government agent trying to set her up? "I don't know if you are legit, crazy, or trying to entrap me," she replied to Citizenfour. Unlike Greenwald, however, Poitras was as intrigued as she was cynical. So intrigued, in fact, that she gave Citizenfour her PGP encryption key and they corresponded for several weeks. She found him an amazing writer—passionate, articulate, and witty.

"Everything I got read like a thriller," Poitras later told *Vanity Fair.*

When he felt secure enough with Poitras, Snowden dropped the first bombshell. He told her that he had a copy of the eighteen-page, top-secret Presidential Policy Directive

20. Issued by President Obama in October 2012, the classified document revealed that the NSA was tapping national and international fiber-optic cables and telephone communications.

"I almost fainted," Poitras recalled.

Citizenfour went on to say that he wanted to meet Poitras, and that he wanted her to work with her friend Glenn Greenwald. Snowden made it clear that he wanted wide, international coverage for his secret documents. He knew, of course, that Poitras was a writer as well as a filmmaker. But he also knew that her reputation—and her value to him—was on the screen, not on paper.

Like Citizenfour, Poitras moved cautiously, but not because she doubted what he had told her. She thought that U.S. intelligence agents were probably monitoring her movements and phone conversations. She didn't want the government to even suspect she was talking to a high-level whistleblower.

✦

In March 2013, two months after Snowden first contacted her, Poitras left Berlin for New York. She assumed that Citzenfour was living in the U.S.—probably somewhere on the East Coast—and she wanted to set up a face-to-face meeting as soon as possible. But first she needed to meet with Greenwald, as Citizenfour had instructed.

When Greenwald landed at JFK airport in New York to deliver a series of lectures about the abuse of civil liberties in the name of the War on Terror, a cryptic cell phone message from Poitras was waiting for him. She was in New York and had something important to share. But not over a phone. Greenwald was both eager to see Poitras again and curious about her coded message. He considered her "one of the most focused, fearless, and independent individuals" he had ever known. If Laura Poitras said she had something important to share, then she did.

The two met the next day in the Yonkers Marriott hotel, where Greenwald was staying. Poitras selected a secluded table in the hotel restaurant. But before she was prepared to say more than "I hope you had a pleasant flight from Rio," she asked Greenwald to either remove the battery from his cell phone or take the phone up to his room. The NSA could remotely activate cell phones and laptops as listening devices, she explained. Just in case Greenwald hadn't heard.

When Greenwald returned from his room, Poitras told him that she had received a string of e-mails from someone called Citizenfour—a man, she concluded—who told her that he had top-secret documents about U.S. spying on Americans and others and who was willing to leak those pages to her on the condition that she would collaborate with Glenn Greenwald. Citizenfour seemed "honest and serious," she said. Then she handed Greenwald two long e-mails.

Greenwald found the messages riveting. His instincts told him the author was authentic. What Citizenfour had written about government snooping and how the NSA was spying on Americans convinced him that Citizenfour was what he claimed to be—a high-level electronic-intelligence operative in the U.S. government. Greenwald didn't realize that Citizenfour and Cincinnatus were the same person. However, before the journalist was willing to take the next step and meet Citizenfour face-to-face, he wanted evidence that Citizenfour actually possessed classified intelligence documents, and that they were authentic.

Greenwald and Poitras agreed to work together. She returned to Berlin and Greenwald to Rio, where he put aside Citizenfour to work on other pressing matters. Cincinnatus, who was sitting on an incendiary and revelatory trove of information, grew impatient. Three weeks after Greenwald returned home, he received an e-mail from Cincinnatus, who had now adopted the code name *Verax*, Latin for "truth teller"—a word commonly used by Plautus, Cicero, Horace, and other Romans when they referred to oracles and gods. Given what Verax was about to do, the moniker once again described how Snowden saw himself.

"I have been working with a friend of yours," he said in his e-mail. "We need to talk urgently." Greenwald now understood that Cincinnatus, Citizenfour, and Verax were the same person. They chatted through OTR (off-the-record), a coded, secure chat line.

"I've been reading you a long time," Verax said. "And I know you'll be aggressive and fearless."

"I'm ready and eager," Greenwald said. "Let's decide what I need to do."

"Get to Hong Kong!"

Greenwald was confused. Like Poitras, he was expecting to meet Verax at some secluded spot in the United States. Hong Kong? Old doubts flooded back. Hong Kong was a city under the control of Communist China. Was Verax working for the Chinese? If so, how? As a spy? A businessman selling U.S. government secrets? Whatever the case, Greenwald thought Hong Kong was a "bizarre" choice.

It wasn't.

Snowden fled to Hong Kong for three specific reasons, he explained later. The citizens of Hong Kong, he reasoned, "have a spirited commitment to free speech and the right of political dissent." And although China has had sovereignty over Hong Kong since 1997, the territory retained a separate legal system with a tradition of free speech. Snowden believed that the citizens of Hong Kong would support his decision to blow the whistle on the United States and to seek protection in their city. He had done his homework. By law, the Hong Kong government could not return anyone who claimed that he would be persecuted. Finally, Snowden believed that Hong Kong was one of the few places in the world that would stand up to Uncle Sam. It would be harder for U.S. intelligence agents to harass him there.

How safe Snowden would be in Hong Kong was far from clear, however. According to Human Rights Watch, Hong Kong authorities had cooperated with the CIA in the past. There was little doubt, the organization believed, that Hong Kong would agree to hand over Snowden to the CIA if requested to do so.

◆

Greenwald didn't press Verax for an explanation of why he chose Hong Kong, for fear of spooking him. Instead, he asked for one good reason why he should spend time, energy, and money to travel halfway around the world for an initial meeting. After helping Greenwald install PGP encryption, Verax gave him twenty-five reasons—the pages of an NSA file describing PRISM.

"Just a very small taste," Verax said. "The tip of the iceberg."

At the urging of Poitras, Snowden had, in early May, sent the same set of PRISM documents to reporter Barton Gellman under the code name *Brassbanner* and, through Gellman, to the *Washington Post*. A Princeton graduate and Rhodes scholar, Gellman had left the newspaper in 2010 to write magazine articles and a bestseller, *Angler: The Cheney Vice-Presidency*. With the Snowden PRISM files in hand, and perhaps smelling another Pulitzer, Gellman returned to the *Post* under a special contract. Although the paper was interested in the story, it refused to allow Gellman to travel to Hong Kong to interview Snowden, proving to Snowden that he was right: the *Washington Post* was fearful and unaggressive.

Poitras had suggested the *Post* to Citizenfour because, she reasoned, if the powerful paper broke the PRISM story, it would be more difficult for the intelligence community to demonize the story than if smaller and less-well-known media published it. Greenwald disagreed with Poitras's independent decision to include the *Post*, which caused a certain amount of friction between the two of them. Although Greenwald respected Barton Gellman, he didn't relish the competition and pressure to be first. More important, he felt that by not consulting with him Poitras had betrayed his trust.

When Greenwald opened the PRISM file, he was stunned. The file read: TOP SECRET . . . COMINT [intelligence communication] . . . NOFORM [not for foreign distribution]. "It was unbelievable," he said later. "There *are no leaks* from the NSA. It was enough to make me hyperventilate . . . I had to stop reading and walk around my house a few times to take in what I had just seen."

Greenwald knew he had to get to Hong Kong fast if he wanted to outscoop the *Washington Post,* assuming it had the guts to run the story. He decided that the *Guardian* would be the best showcase for the Verax leaks—if Verax was credible and his documents authentic. The British daily had a UK circulation of just under 200,000, but an online readership of as many as nine million. It had bureaus in Chicago, Washington, and New York. Important to Greenwald, the *Guardian* "had a longstanding liberal and anti-establishment approach to journalism."

As a new columnist for the *Guardian,* Greenwald had cultivated a comfortable working relationship with the *Guardian's* U.S. editor, Janine Gibson, who was British. He had been a popular columnist for the online news magazine *Salon,* and the *Guardian* was counting on him to bring his more than one million *Salon* followers with him. The newspaper gave him a great deal of editorial independence, unless it anticipated legal problems with a particular article. In such a case, the newspaper would have the right to insist on editorial changes.

Greenwald called Gibson from Rio. "Janine," he began, "I have a huge story." She cut him off. "Not over the phone," she warned. Two days later, Greenwald was sitting in the *Guardian's* loft-style office in SoHo, reviewing the PRISM documents on his PGP-secure computer with Gibson. Mesmerized by the material, she told Greenwald that she wanted to be involved in publishing it, pending approval by the *Guardian's* editor-in-chief in London. And once she secured this approval, the paper would pay for his trip to Hong Kong.

As Snowden had done with Poitras, Gibson laid down a

condition. Greenwald would have to work with Ewan Mac-Askill, a twenty-one-year veteran political reporter at the *Guardian*. MacAskill was a seasoned newsman with a stint as a foreign correspondent under his belt. He had a reputation for integrity and reliability, and was highly respected by the paper's top management in London, where Greenwald was barely known. Adding MacAskill to the team, Gibson argued, would virtually ensure a nod from London. Mac-Askill's primary job would be to evaluate Verax, to determine if he was credible and could deliver the goods. If so, Mac-Askill would email Gibson from Hong Kong and say, "The Guinness is good."

✦

Neither Greenwald nor Poitras was happy with Gibson's demand. Snowden was expecting two reporters, not three. They were afraid that the surprise would drive Snowden back into his shell. With those reservations gnawing at them, Greenwald and Poitras—with MacAskill in tow—boarded a Cathay Pacific flight from New York to Hong Kong the next day, June 1, 2013, six months after Cincinnatus first approached Greenwald. By that time, both Poitras and Greenwald knew their source's real name. Snowden had revealed himself to Poitras as a measure of good faith. But neither Poitras nor Greenwald knew what he looked like.

"I thought he must be a pretty senior bureaucrat," Greenwald later recalled. "Probably 60-odd, wearing a blue blazer with shiny gold buttons, receding grey hair, sensible black shoes, spectacles, a club tie. Perhaps he was the CIA's station chief in Hong Kong."

During the flight, Poitras gave Greenwald a thumb drive containing thousands of classified documents that Snowden had sent her. Greenwald read as many as he could for the next sixteen hours in the air. The majority of the files were marked "top secret," and most of those were labeled "FVEY" (five eyes), meaning that they could only be distributed to NSA officials and their four foreign partners—Great Britain, Canada, Australia, and New Zealand. As cynical as Greenwald was, he found many of the documents shocking. As he put it, he was both overwhelmed with the detail and stunned by the scope of NSA's worldwide spying. He also found Snowden's documents well organized—"folders and then sub-folders, and sub-sub-folders"—the work of a sophisticated, astute man.

Snowden was concerned that Greenwald and Poitras might be tailed to his hotel, so he meticulously planned a cloak-and-dagger introduction. He and the reporters would meet late morning at the deluxe Mira Hotel, which was attached to a shopping mall in the heart of Hong Kong's Kowloon tourist district. Holding a Rubik's Cube, Snowden would be sitting next to a large plastic alligator in a quiet but open hallway halfway between the hotel restaurant and the hotel shopping mall. Greenwald would identify himself by asking: "What time does the restaurant open?" Snowden would answer: "At noon, but don't go in there, the food sucks."

Greenwald recalled later that when he saw how young Snowden was, he was flabbergasted. Dressed in a T-shirt, jeans, and sneakers, Snowden, who was almost twenty-nine, looked like a teenager. "I had expected a sixty-year-old, grizzled veteran, someone in the high echelons of the intelligence service," Greenwald recalled. "I thought 'This is going to be a wasted trip.'"

When Greenwald recovered from the visual shock and the coded introductions were over, the young man formally identified himself as "Ed" Snowden and led Greenwald, Poitras, and MacAskill to the hotel elevator and up to Room 1014.

"Sorry," he said as he led them in. "It's a bit messy."

It was a small, cluttered, $330-a-night room with a view of Kowloon Park below. There was a bed, table and chairs, television, bathroom; dirty plates, bowls of half-eaten noodles and soiled clothes were strewn around. A copy of *Angler,* Gellman's biography of Dick Cheney, sat on a table next to the bed.

If the presence of MacAskill disturbed Snowden, he didn't show it. According to Greenwald, "He radiated a sense of tranquility and equanimity. He had reached a rock-like place of inner certainty. Here, nothing could touch him."

Although tranquil, Snowden took no chances. Before the taped interview began, he stacked pillows against the door to soundproof it. Whenever he consulted a computer for specific information, he placed a red hood over his head and the keyboard, saying that government agents could set up hidden cameras that would capture his secret passwords as he typed them in. He refused MacAskill's request to record the interview on his iPhone because, he explained, the NSA would be able to hear and copy the entire interview. Poitras placed the iPhone in the refrigerator in her room, just down the hall.

Poitras quickly set up her tripod and video camera, then miked Snowden and Greenwald, who would be the first to interview him. After vetting Snowden on camera—it took five hours—MacAskill emailed Gibson in New York and said "The Guinness is good." Then he and Greenwald began writing a series of articles for the *Guardian* while Poitras began editing a twelve-minute video interview in which Snowden identified himself as the anonymous NSA whistleblower. The Poitras interview ended with Snowden quoting Benjamin Franklin: "Those who surrender freedom for security will not have, nor do they deserve, either one."

It is important to note here that Snowden didn't hand over every classified NSA document that he had downloaded onto a thumb drive. "There are all sorts of documents that would have made a big impact that I didn't turn over," he said, "because harming people isn't my goal. Transparency is."

The articles and the video hit the shores of the unsuspecting world like a late spring tsunami, sending the White House and 10 Downing Street scurrying for cover. Greenwald was so worried he might be arrested if he landed at JFK airport in New York that he booked his flight back to Rio through Dubai in the United Arab Emirates.

5

WHOM TO TELL
Silkwood

Karen Silkwood first blew the whistle to her superiors in Washington, D.C., in late September 1974. It was ten weeks before she would die and nine years before Edward Snowden would be born. The legislative office of the Oil, Chemical and Atomic Workers Union had invited the officers of Local 5-283 to present their health and safety concerns to a panel of AEC bureaucrats. It was a bold move.

As the government's watchdog over its nuclear contractors, the AEC had real authority. It could fine contractors for health and safety violations or terminate their contracts if commission inspectors found their plants or laboratories too unhealthy or too dangerous to remain open. In going directly to the top of the AEC, the union was bypassing the commission's regional office in Chicago. Under the leadership of James Klepper, the Midwest office was directly responsible for oversight of the Kerr-McGee Cimarron plant. As such, the Chicago office was a dismal and dangerous failure.

Silkwood came to Washington armed with her spiral notebook filled with the health and safety violations she had found at the plant during the previous two months. The dated entries described in detail the almost daily toxic spills and air contaminations, as well as management's negligence and cover-ups—all based on personal observations and interviews with her fellow workers.

It is not clear precisely what OCAW's legislative office in D.C. hoped to accomplish by calling a rare face-to-face meeting with AEC brass behind the back of Kerr-McGee, other than to get another union complaint on the record at the highest level. What was clear, however, was that the AEC and Kerr-McGee had been cozy bedfellows for more than twenty-five years. Klepper's *scheduled* inspections of the Cimarron plant bordered on ludicrous. Plant managers knew about the visits so far in advance that they had plenty of time to "polish the silver"—tidy up the plant, properly store its 800 pounds of radioactive plutonium, and make sure that all air filters were fresh, all required alarms were working, and all workers who were required to wear respirators were actually wearing them. Workers were also warned not to voluntarily speak to AEC investigators.

If the scheduled inspections were a joke, Klepper's *unannounced* inspections were pure fraud. Plant managers knew of "surprise" visit days in advance so they had plenty of time to prepare. When workers got an urgent order to get their work areas shipshape and up to safety standards, they all knew a surprise inspection was just around the corner. And right before the AEC inspectors arrived at the plant, an announcement came over the PA system, "They're here!"

The OCAW Crescent team (Jack Tice, Karen Silkwood, and Jerry Brewer) met with the union's legislative team (Tony Mazzocchi and Steve Wodka) in OCAW's office across the street from the *Washington Post* building. Wodka was a newly minted lawyer. Mazzocchi was a union-management war veteran and had the scars to prove it. He would learn several months after the meeting with the Crescent team that the CIA had placed a listening device behind his kitchen clock. The location was an inspired choice. It was in their kitchen that Mazzocchi and his wife talked about his union problems and plans.

Mazzocchi explained to the Crescent team that they were scheduled to meet with an AEC panel the following day. He asked them to review their laundry list of issues with him and Wodka. What he and Wodka heard was all too familiar—corporate deceit, gross negligence, and AEC collusion. All in the name of Cold War urgency.

At the end of the preparatory meeting, almost as an afterthought, Silkwood told Mazzocchi and Wodka that she had stumbled on another problem at the plant and wondered if she should mention it to the AEC the next day. Someone at the plant, she said, was doctoring quality-control negatives that showed defects in the fuel rods destined for the AEC's experimental nuclear reactor in Hanford, Washington. Maybe it was important, she thought.

✦

It wasn't clear to nuclear scientists in 1974 just how dangerous it would be if fuel rods filled with plutonium pellets leaked radiation inside the Westinghouse fast-flux, experimental nuclear reactor in Hanford. The scientists all seemed to agree, however, that defective fuel rods should be taken seriously, and they posited three possible scenarios. In the first, the radiation released from defective fuel rods inside the nuclear reactor would simply be absorbed into the solution that cooled it. That would pose no risk. In the second scenario, the reactor would have to be shut down, the radioactive solution safely siphoned off and disposed of, and the leaking rods replaced. That would be expensive, but not dangerous. In the third scenario, the leaking fuel rods could cause a criticality accident that would release radiation that could contaminate the environment for years to come and endanger the health and lives of those living near the Westinghouse plant.

OCAW welcomed Silkwood's information. The union was struggling with declining membership. Its 185,000 atomic workers in the United States and Canada were squeezed between their union and the government-controlled nuclear industry. At stake were their jobs. If the union made too many demands, corporations like Kerr-McGee would shut their plants. Kerr-McGee took full advantage of its employees' fear of losing their jobs, and their anger at Karen Silkwood for rocking the boat. A month before Silkwood left Crescent for the Washington meeting, a nonunion worker at the plant launched a drive to have the National Labor Relations Board (NLRB) decertify OCAW as the bargaining agent for plant workers, both union and nonunion. OCAW suspected—but could not prove—that Kerr-McGee management was behind the decertification drive. And OCAW also suspected—but could not prove—that the company had spies inside the union who reported Local 5-283's plans to management. Kerr-McGee apparently knew, for example— either from spies or from a tip from the AEC itself—that the local was secretly planning a trip to Washington at the end of September.

The NLRB required that at least 30 percent of a plant's workers sign a petition requesting decertification before the NLRB would agree to supervise a decertification vote. More than one-third of Kerr-McGee's workers had signed such a petition. And since the current union-management contract was due to expire in December, the NLRB had set the decertification ballot for October 16. This was bad news for Local 5-283. Unless it could prove to Kerr-McGee workers that the union made a difference in their working conditions, the union would almost certainly lose the vote. And if the union was decertified in October, workers would end up with a weak, two-year contract in December.

For most workers, however, a weak contract was better than no job.

When Silkwood told Mazzocchi and Wodka in Washington that she would be willing to collect records proving quality-control tampering, Jerry Brewer argued against it. If Silkwood were caught collecting the records, he reasoned, Kerr-McGee would prosecute her for theft and the union would come under heavy fire as an accomplice. Mazzocchi seemed to agree with Brewer but left the door cracked. He told Silkwood not to bring up the defective-fuel-rod issue during the meeting with the AEC the following day. It was a special issue, he said, and it should be handled separately.

If Silkwood surprised Mazzocchi with her quality-control-tampering allegation, Mazzocchi shocked Silkwood. Almost as an afterthought, he mentioned during the preparatory meeting that there was a link between plutonium and cancer. His matter-of-fact remark rattled Silkwood. She was bright, had attended college, and had been working in a scientific laboratory with plutonium for two years. No one at Kerr-McGee or the AEC had told her during her training, or afterwards, that plutonium was carcinogenic. No one had taken an anatomical chart, pointed to lungs, liver, lymph nodes, and bones, and said that plutonium could cause cancer in those places in twenty-five or thirty years. The news both angered and frightened her. And for good reason.

Karen Silkwood had worked in a room contaminated with airborne plutonium without a respirator just two months earlier. All her tests had come up positive. She had plutonium in her body. Now she had to wonder: would it slowly kill her?

◆

The three OCAW officers from Local 5-283 and Steve Wodka met with John Davis, deputy director of AEC field operations, and a handful of other commission officials at their national headquarters in Bethesda, Maryland, at the end of September 1974. Davis was responsible for the Chicago regional office and its four inspectors. Wodka explained to the panel why OCAW had asked for the unprecedented meeting. He accused Kerr-McGee of failing to keep levels of exposure to plutonium as low as practicable, provide proper hygienic facilities, educate and train workers adequately, and monitor worker exposure.

Next, Silkwood presented thirty-nine specific examples to illustrate Wodka's general allegations. The most serious dealt with respirators, defective warning alarms, and careless handling of radioactive plutonium. When alarms sounded a warning that an area was contaminated, Silkwood told the AEC panel, the management frequently turned the alarms off and told workers to keep working. It was only a test, they said.

Radioactive plutonium samples were stored in desk drawers or out in the open on a shelf, Silkwood explained. They could be easily stolen or tossed into the garbage by mistake. Workers not wearing respirators were not warned that their work area was contaminated. They breathed radioactive air, as she had. Furthermore, workers were ordered to wear respirators for up to twelve straight hours, and up to ten days in a row. Such extended use of respirators was a violation of AEC guidelines. Respirators induce fatigue and fatigue causes dangerous mistakes.

Finally, Silkwood pointed out, there was no routine maintenance of respirators at the Cimarron plant, even after extended use. As a result, some filters leaked or were clogged. Respirator filters were not replaced regularly as required by the AEC. Dirty, clogged filters were reused to save money, workers complained.

The respirator issue was especially troubling. Dr. Karl Z. Morgan, the reputed "father of health physics," would testify during the Silkwood family's negligence suit against Kerr-McGee five years after the OCAW-AEC meeting in Bethesda: "To allow someone to continue over a period of time—even more than one hour—using these safety masks, sometimes only partially safe masks, is inexcusable and irresponsible . . . callous, willful, wanton negligence." That trial testimony was not only a slap in the face of Kerr-McGee. It was a frontal attack on the AEC itself. Dr. Morgan accused the commission of the same "inexcusable and irresponsible

. . . callous, willful, wanton negligence" as Kerr–McGee, either by allowing the company to employ such hazardous practices or by looking the other way.

After the Bethesda meeting, John Davis promised Wodka that he would see to it that each of the thirty-nine allegations was thoroughly investigated. Wodka was skeptical. He asked Davis not to tip off Kerr–McGee that the commission was investigating union complaints, or to share with Kerr–Mc-Gee the information he had heard at the meeting. And since Wodka didn't trust Davis's regional AEC investigators who monitored and inspected the Cimarron plant, he went one step further. He asked Davis to assign investigators who were not the regular inspectors from the AEC's regional office in Chicago. It was all Wodka could do at the moment, and he wasn't terribly hopeful that anything meaningful would happen to improve health and safety at the Kerr–McGee nuclear plant.

Mazzocchi had his own plan. After the meeting with the AEC panel, he asked Silkwood to step into his office. He told her that quality-control tampering was serious, and that he wanted to leak Kerr–McGee documents proving the fraud to the *New York Times*. He hoped to do that, he told Silkwood, just before contract negotiations with Kerr–McGee began to heat up. A *Times* exposé, he explained, would apply the kind of national pressure on Kerr–McGee that a struggling local couldn't. The *Times* would need specifics, he warned Silkwood. Which fuel rods were unsafe and why. Their weld numbers. When the defects were identified. Who was covering up. Most important, Mazzocchi told Silkwood, the *Times* would expect to receive samples of the doctored quality-control negatives.

"I can't get them," Silkwood said.

Mazzocchi warned Silkwood that she had to work quietly and unobtrusively and not tell anyone about her undercover assignment, not even Tice or Brewer. She should report only to Steve Wodka. Silkwood said she understood.

✦

The day after the AEC meeting, Silkwood returned to Crescent with a mission—to steal doctored quality-control negatives and supporting documents and hide them. As requested, she reported to Wodka. In a phone call two weeks after she returned home—which Wodka recorded with Silkwood's permission—she said, "They are still passing high welds no matter what the picture looks like. . . . We grind down too far. And I've got a weld I would love for you to see, just how far they ground it down till we lost the weld, trying to get rid of the voids and inclusions and cracks."

Wodka and Mazzocchi both understood that their plan to expose the shoddy and potentially dangerous plutonium/uranium pellet manufacturing at the Kerr-McGee Cimarron plant was contingent on the local defeating the decertification vote. In hopes of winning an upset victory, they planned to drop a bombshell. If atomic workers like Karen Silkwood didn't know that plutonium causes cancer, how would they react if they found out from experts that it did? And what if they found out that Kerr-McGee and the AEC, which had approved the corporation's training manual, had deliberately hidden that fact from them?

On October 10, three weeks after Silkwood returned from Washington and six days before the decertification ballot, Wodka invited Dean Abrahamson and Donald Geesaman, nuclear scientists on the faculty of the University of Minnesota, to talk to Kerr-McGee union and nonunion workers alike about the health hazards of radioactive plutonium. Both scientists deeply distrusted the AEC, its muzzled nuclear physicists, and the commission's so-called contamination "safe" limits.

Abrahamson and Geesaman scared the complacency right out of the Cimarron plant rank-and-file workers during their rotating lectures. Plutonium gets into the air in the plant as either fine dust or mist. You breathe the insoluble dust in through your nose or mouth. It goes down your windpipe into your lungs. Or into your esophagus and stomach. And it sits there, bombarding your organs with radioactive particles, for the rest of your life. The radioactive mist, the scientists explained, is dissolved in your blood and settles mainly in your liver and bones. No one knows how much plutonium will cause cancer, or when, or where—in the lungs, throat, stomach, liver, bones. The AEC's so-called safe limits were grossly understated and basically deceitful.

The strategy worked. Cimarron plant workers voted 80 to 61 to keep the OCAW as its bargaining agent. It was now up to Karen Silkwood to deliver the negatives and documents, as promised, to the *New York Times* and its investigative reporter David Burnham.

The date, time, and location for the meeting were set: November 13. Early evening. Holiday Inn Northwest. Oklahoma City. Silkwood told Wodka that she would be ready.

6

WHY

Snowden

Less than a week after Glenn Greenwald, Laura Poitras, and Ewan MacAskill touched down in Hong Kong, the *Guardian* published four major articles in a row based on the Snowden leaks. Those news stories, published between June 5 and June 8, 2013, portrayed the NSA as a giant rogue vacuum cleaner, indiscriminately sucking in personal data from around the world. The exposés landed on Washington and London like napalm. The *Guardian* editors were nervous: would the paper be dragged into court? Would the U.S. government shut down its Chicago, Washington, and New York offices?

A summary of the four *Guardian* articles—the tip of the iceberg, as Snowden called them—helps explain *why* Edward Snowden felt compelled to leak the highly classified documents that those articles were based on.

✦

The first article, written by Greenwald and published on June 5, 2013, began: "The National Security Agency is currently collecting the telephone electronic records of millions of U.S. customers of Verizon, one of America's largest telecommunication providers, under a top secret court order." The article revealed a classified decision of the U.S. Foreign Intelligence Surveillance Court (FISC) issued on April 12, 2013, headed "TOP SECRET//SI//NOFORN." (SI means special intelligence. NOFORN means not for foreign distribution.)

Congress created the court in 1978, according to a provision of the U.S. Foreign Intelligence Surveillance Act, to process intelligence agency requests for surveillance warrants on U.S. citizens. Congress made FISC the quasi "supreme court" for the intelligence community by giving it the sole power to decide which surveillance requests were constitutional and/or legal, and which were not. Critics have called FISC a kangaroo court, stuffed with handpicked hawks unlikely to challenge broad surveillance requests approved by the president of the United States. Unlike the U.S. Supreme Court, FISC's appointed arbiters are not publicly vetted. Its deliberations are closed to the public and the media. And its decisions and minutes are classified top secret.

Greenwald's *Guardian* article explained the significance of the FISC ruling: "The document shows for the first time that under the Obama administration the communication records of millions of U.S. citizens are being collected indiscriminately, regardless of whether they are suspected of any wrongdoing."

The classified April 2013 FISC ruling, signed by Judge Roger Vinson, ordered Verizon to give the NSA electronic copies of "all call detail records." To skirt privacy laws, FISC defined those records as "metadata" (transactional information), not personal data, which was what they actually were. The court further ordered Verizon to provide data on all foreign and domestic phone calls on an "ongoing, daily basis." In essence, FISC ruled that NSA's collection, analysis, and use of the phone conversations of Americans did not violate the U.S. Criminal Code or the privacy concerns of the Fourth Amendment, which states, "The right of the people to be secure in their persons, houses, papers, and effects, against unreasonable searches and seizures, shall not be violated, and no warrants shall issue, but upon probable cause, supported by oath or affirmation, and particularly describing the place to be searched, and the persons or things to be seized."

FISC justified its granting of limitless telephone spying on Verizon's customers as a valid extension of a controversial provision in the Patriot Act passed by Congress after 9/11. Section 215 of the act significantly lowered the bar on the probable cause needed for the intelligence community to collect data on private citizens. Because all FISC decisions are classified top secret, no one could challenge its blanket grant to the NSA to collect telephone communications of innocent Americans without having to describe, in each case, "the place to be searched and the persons or things to be seized."

✦

The second major article, coauthored by Greenwald and MacAskill and published in the *Guardian* on June 6, 2013, exposed PRISM, one of the NSA's most successful secret data-gathering programs targeting private citizens. The *Guard-*

ian's headline read: "The National Security Agency has obtained direct access to the systems of Google, Facebook, Apple and other internet giants." James Clapper, the U.S. director of national intelligence, defended PRISM. "Information collected under this program is among the most important and valuable intelligence information we collect," he said, "and is used to protect our nation from a wide variety of threats."

According to Snowden's classified documents, the PRISM program, which began with Microsoft in 2007, was unique because the NSA had secret court authority to directly tap the servers of private Internet companies without having to request permission from the court to justify each and every search. The source for the PRISM stories was highly unusual—a top-secret PowerPoint slide presentation that the NSA apparently used to teach its intelligence operatives how to directly access specific private Internet servers.

One of the PowerPoint's forty-one slides, labeled "Prism Collection Details," presents a list of NSA's providers. Besides Google, Facebook, and Apple, the slide names Yahoo, PalTalk, YouTube, Microsoft Hotmail, Skype, and AOL. (The NSA planned to add Dropbox to its list of surveillance targets as well.) The same slide goes on to explain what NSA intelligence operatives could expect to reap from the PRISM data collection: e-mails, chats (video and voice), photos, stored data and files, file transfers, videoconferencing, notification of target logins, online social networking, and special user requests. The PRISM program documents suggested that the Internet companies cooperated willingly. If so, it would mean that nearly all of Silicon Valley was working for the NSA.

The original idea behind PRISM was to intercept the communications of potential terrorists and their supporters. But the NSA soon succumbed to the temptation to include the communications of Americans who were not terrorist suspects and who had no known association with suspected terrorist organizations.

In essence, FISC had given the NSA the authority to spy on the entire world of telephone and Internet communication in collaboration with its foreign partners, without obtaining prior court-ordered warrants. Besides unwitting, ordinary Americans, PRISM's targets included world leaders and friends such as German chancellor Angela Merkel, who let her fellow Germans—and the rest of the world—know just how outraged she was that the United States was listening to her private cell phone calls.

The official response to the PRISM stories published by the *Guardian*—and by the *Washington Post*—was to run for cover. President Obama defended NSA's snoop programs. "You can't have 100% security and also have 100% privacy and no inconvenience," he said. Internet companies named in the PRISM slides—like Facebook and Google—expressed public outrage. Google proclaimed, "Any suggestion that Google is disclosing information about our users' Internet activity on such a scale is false." And Facebook claimed, "We haven't heard of PRISM before yesterday."

Snowden didn't buy the denials. "[They] went through several revisions," he told the *Guardian*. "It became more and more clear that they were misleading and included identical, specific language across companies."

It will take years, if ever, to unravel the full operating details of PRISM, not to mention its legality and constitutionality, and who was lying. Those Internet companies charged with aiding and abetting NSA privacy invasions will try to hide behind semantics such as private information versus metadata; direct versus indirect access to servers; and broad surveillance versus individual requests. It is easy to imagine a day when the public will either be fed up or bored with the hairsplitting, and the issue of culpability will fade away.

✦

The third major article in the *Guardian*, also written by Greenwald and MacAskill, was an exposé of a top-secret NSA program code named BOUNDLESS INFORMANT. An ongoing operation, it was a data-mining tool that provided NSA analysts with summaries of data records (so-called metadata) retrieved from 504 separate international data collection pools, including sources inside the United States. The major targets of the worldwide program, by volume, were Iran, Pakistan, Jordan, and Egypt in the Middle East; Germany and France in Western Europe; and Brazil in South America.

The NSA made it easy for Greenwald and other journalists to explain the scope of BOUNDLESS INFORMANT. Among Snowden's classified documents was a color-coded map showing which countries the NSA was spying on, as well as how much metadata it was collecting on each country each day. For example, the map showed that BOUNDLESS INFORMANT had retrieved nearly three billion pieces of data from inside the United States during a one-month period beginning on March 8, 2013.

In that same month it had also captured more than five hundred million pieces of telephone and Internet data in Germany, NSA's most important European target.

Snowden's leaking of the BOUNDLESS INFORMANT operation mortified the NSA. The classified documents showed that NSA officials had been lying to Congress for years, repeatedly testifying that the agency didn't know, or couldn't calculate, how many American phone calls and e-mails it was intercepting. BOUNDLESS INFORMANT revealed the number by hour, by day, by month.

✦

The fourth major article exposed the secret snooping of NSA's biggest and most important foreign partner, GCHQ (Government Communications Headquarters). GCHQ was Britain's electronic eavesdropping and security agency. Ewan MacAskill uncovered the GCHQ snooping program, TEMPORA, during his ninety-minute interview with Snowden in Hong Kong, the day after Greenwald had finished his five-hour interview. MacAskill was shocked. GCHQ and the NSA were PRISM partners.

Snowden had managed to copy fifty-thousand GCHQ files from NSA data banks. Those files revealed for the first time how GCHQ had tapped several hundred transatlantic cables and how, with the help of NSA's PRISM program, it was spying on British citizens who were not suspected terrorists. Because MacAskill had uncovered the story in the Snowden documents, Greenwald and Poitras agreed to let him and his British team develop the GCHQ-NSA connection for the *Guardian*.

Beginning in June 2010, three years before Snowden blew the whistle, the NSA began sharing with GCHQ PRISM's access to the servers of the nine major Internet companies. That link allowed the British intelligence agency to spy on the private communications of British citizens, just as the NSA was spying on Americans. To make the PRISM-sharing possible, the NSA had to design special programs and provide special training courses to teach British intelligence agents how to use them. According to the secret GCHQ files leaked by Snowden, the British spy agency between 2010 and 2013 had generated 197 intelligence reports that were based on PRISM information. In return, GCHQ shared its advanced technology with the NSA.

Geographically, Great Britain is ideally located to snoop on the world. Its position on the eastern edge of the Atlantic makes it an Internet hub. According to author Luke Harding, "As much as 25% of the world's current internet traffic crosses British territory via cables, en route between the United States, Europe, Africa, and all points east." Furthermore, GHCQ's headquarters in Cheltenham in southwest England is close to major transatlantic cables. It is relatively cheap and easy to tap them. Joined by the United States on the west side of the Atlantic, the two countries host most of the world's Internet traffic.

The NSA and GCHQ teamed up to develop the biggest and most sophisticated computerized Internet buffer in the world to store Internet data. Intelligence analysts and data miners would then sort through the vast pool of digital communications at GHCQ's new Regional Processing Center. At its peak, TEMPORA was tapping more than two hundred fiber-optic cables. The volume of data was heavy. In one twenty-four-hour period, for example, TEMPORA processed and stored more than thirty-nine billion events (phone calls or e-mails). This far exceeded what the NSA could process in a single day. GCHQ made these intercepts available to NSA's 850,000 employees and contract workers like Edward Snowden. To sift the data, the NSA developed 30,000 "triggers" or filters. GCHQ had 40,000 such triggers. TEMPORA stored data up to thirty days to give intelligence analysts time to record, categorize, and analyze content.

NSA's access to GCHQ's data banks didn't come cheaply. The United States paid the British intelligence agency more than 175 million pounds between 2009 and 2012 to develop and sustain TEMPORA and their mutual spy operations, code-named Samuel Pepys, Big Piggy, Bad Wolf, Egotistical Giraffe, and Olympia. That put enormous pressure on GCHQ to keep up with the growing sophistication and diversity of world communications.

One Snowden leak sent shock waves across the English Channel. GCHQ had bugged the foreign leaders attending two G-20 summit meetings hosted in London in 2009. The spy agency had managed to hack the delegates' passwords and penetrate their BlackBerrys.

◆

When Edward Snowden blew the whistle on FISC, PRISM, BOUNDLESS INFORMANT, and GCHQ—as well as other NSA spy programs with code names like Thin Thread, Trailblazer, Turbulence, Muscular, Fairview, and Bullrun—he earned a place at the top of the Justice Department's Most Wanted list.

Why did he do it? Why take the risk? Why not look the other way, like most of his NSA colleagues?

For one thing, the motives for such actions tend to be mixed because both the mind and the heart are involved in such an important decision. As a result, whistleblowers don't always completely understand why they do something significant. There are buried feelings and hidden triggers of which they either are unaware, or cannot access, because they are somehow perceived as threatening. Simply put, not only are we capable of lying; we are also quite accomplished at lying to ourselves.

From his first interview in Hong Kong with Glenn Greenwald to a string of televised statements and interviews from Hong Kong and Moscow, Edward Snowden clearly explained his reasons for leaking classified documents on such widespread, sensitive, and embarrassing spy programs. He has never veered from his original story:

> "My sole purpose is to inform the public as to that which is done in their name and that which is done against them" . . . .
>
> The U.S. government, in conspiracy with client states, chiefest among them the Five Eyes—[the United States,] the United Kingdom, Canada, Australia, and New Zealand—have inflicted upon the world a system of secret, pervasive surveillance from which there is no refuge. They protect their domestic systems from the oversight of citizenry through classification and lies, and shield themselves from outrage in the event of leaks by overemphasizing [the] limited protection they choose to grant the governed. . . .

The NSA has built an infrastructure that allows it to intercept almost everything . . . from everybody, everywhere and to store it indefinitely. . . . With this capability, the vast majority of human communications are automatically ingested without targeting. If I wanted to see your e-mails, or your wife's phone, all I have to do is use intercepts. I can get your e-mails, passwords, phone records, credit cards. . . .

I became aware of just how invasive U.S. surveillance capabilities had become. . . . I realized the true breadth of this system. And almost nobody knew it was happening. . . . I felt it would be wrong to, in effect, help conceal all of this from the public. . . .

I have gone to the darkest corners of government, and what they fear is light. . . .

Every person remembers some moment in their life where they witnessed some injustice, big or small, and looked away, because the consequences of intervening seemed too intimidating. But there's a limit to the amount of incivility and inequality and inhumanity that each individual can tolerate. I crossed that line. . . .

Citizenship carries with it a duty to first police one's own government before seeking to correct others. . . . If you're not acting on your beliefs, then they probably aren't real. . . . I don't want to be a person who remains afraid to act in defense of my principles. . . .

I don't want to destroy these systems, but to allow the public to decide whether they should go on. . . . I will be satisfied if the federation of secret law, unequal pardon, and irresistible executive powers that rule the world that I love are revealed for even a second. . . .

I want to spark a worldwide debate about privacy, Internet freedom, and the dangers of state surveillance. . . .

I do not want to live in a world where we have no privacy and freedom, where the unique value of the Internet is snuffed out. . . .

I don't want to be a person who remains afraid to act in defense of my principles. . . .

I know it's the right thing to do."

7

WHY

Silkwood

Karen Silkwood didn't have a Glenn Greenwald to probe her motivation for blowing the whistle on Kerr-McGee for health and safety violations and on the AEC for looking the other way. Had Silkwood lived to deliver her stolen documents to David Burnham, the *New York Times* reporter would have aggressively questioned her motivation, as Greenwald had challenged Snowden's. As the reporter who broke the Serpico story three years before Silkwood's death and had written a complicated narrative of New York Police Department corruption, Burnham knew his reputation and that of his newspaper were at stake. But because Silkwood was killed before she could deliver her documents to Burnham or give media interviews as Snowden had, we can only deduce her motives from what she did and what she said.

What she did was to collect closely held, private information on health and safety violations and quality-control fraud at the Kerr-McGee Cimarron plant. She did this as a local union representative and at the request of her international union. She agreed to snoop and steal sensitive documents because it was clear—from the day she reluctantly joined the OCAW picket line to the last union meeting she attended at the Hub Café on the night she was killed—that she was deeply concerned about the health and safety of her fellow workers. She expressed that concern in a recorded phone call to Steve Wodka soon after she returned to the Cimarron plant from her meeting with the AEC in Bethesda: "We got eighteen and nineteen year old boys, you know. . . . They didn't have any schooling, so they don't understand what radiation is . . . Steve, they don't understand."

Besides being concerned about the health and safety of her fellow workers, Silkwood was concerned about the way the Kerr-McGee plant was contaminating the Cimarron River and the environment. She knew about the scrap recovery program at the Cimarron plant and how untrained workers sorted plant waste into "keepers" and "throwers." The throwers were buried after workers logged the amount of plutonium they were tossing out with the item. Keepers would pass through ion exchange, where the plutonium was saved and all other metal discarded. The AEC charged Kerr-McGee a fee for the discarded or lost plutonium. In the beginning, Kerr-McGee found it cheaper to bury the plutonium-contaminated items than to clean off the plutonium. But as the AEC raised the price of the metal, Kerr-McGee found more and more keepers.

The dumping of plutonium-contaminated waste in a pond behind the plant and the burying of "hot" items in a nearby dump had environmental consequences. The radioactive contamination seeped into the Cimarron River, a source of local drinking water. There was at least one major fish kill in the river below the plant. Kerr-McGee health physicists and others—wearing moon suits and protective booties and gloves—scooped up hundreds of dead fish in the middle of the night and secretly buried them. The fish funeral soon became an open secret.

Kerr-McGee's and the AEC's lack of concern about the environment and worker health and safety made Silkwood angry. And anger is a compelling, and blinding force. She was angry because Kerr-McGee and the AEC had deceived her and continued to lie to their nuclear workers. She was angry because they conveniently forgot to tell her (and them) that airborne plutonium particles inhaled into the lungs and insoluble radioactive mist absorbed by the body can, and most likely will, cause cancer if one lives long enough. She was angry because Kerr-McGee and the AEC hid from the public how severely they were polluting the Cimarron River and the surrounding environment. Would the men, women, and children who lived near the plant, drank the local water, and breathed the local air develop lung, liver, or bone cancer someday?

Most important, Silkwood had breathed plutonium into her lungs while working at the plant, and she believed this contamination with insoluble plutonium, some of which ended up in her stomach, had been deliberate. As radiation experts testified in 1979 at the Silkwood family's negligence lawsuit against Kerr-McGee—Karen Gay Silkwood was "married to cancer."

There is no doubt that Silkwood blamed either Kerr-McGee management or one of her fellow workers for her deliberate contamination, which began four months before she died. Less than an hour before her death, she told her friend Wanda Jean Young, "I can't believe who would do such a thing like that [to me]. It's got to be someone who works at Kerr-McGee." Young would later tell investigators that Silkwood was passionate about "kicking their ass."

✦

It was no coincidence that Silkwood's last known words were spoken to Jean Young, who had heard Dr. Abrahamson's lecture on the dangers of radiation. Like Silkwood, Young had been shocked to learn about the plutonium-cancer connection. Young herself had been severely contaminated a month after the talk. It was Silkwood who found the source of that radiation and learned that Kerr-McGee management had violated AEC regulations and covered it up.

After the health physics workers inspected the lab where Young had been working, Silkwood discovered holes in five sealed glove-box gloves, through which plutonium particles had escaped. Young had breathed contaminated air for up to ten straight hours without a respirator.

"Instead of getting the staff out of the room after they found out it was hot," Silkwood told Wodka in a recorded phone call, "the supervisor overruled health physics and he said: 'I want those gloves changed . . . so that we can continue with production.'" Silkwood continued, "They didn't tell them to get a nasal smear. They didn't say *one* thing to them, and they were in there from ten till eight . . . in that air."

Silkwood advised Young to get a nasal smear. Young was so scared that as soon as she got to the health physics office she paged Silkwood to join her. Silkwood found her friend crying. As the health physics supervisor took the nasal smear with a piece of gauze on a wooden strip, he told Young not to worry, that all the plutonium probably got cleaned out. "You don't *know* that," Young fired back. "I could have gotten some of that down into my lungs."

Silkwood told Wodka, "Steve, this shit is going on every day so [plutonium] accumulates, doesn't it?"

"It sure as hell does," Wodka said.

When the independent laboratory results arrived a week later, they showed that Young's contamination with airborne plutonium was serious—well beyond the so-called safe limits established by the AEC.

◆

Was Karen Silkwood so angry that she wanted to destroy Kerr-McGee and the AEC? She was certainly not the rabid antinuke activist that the FBI and her enemies tried to make her out to be. There is nothing to suggest that she was against nuclear power. Rather, she rallied against abuse, fraud, and deceit in the AEC-sponsored nuclear industry. Like Edward Snowden, Silkwood wanted to pierce the veil of secrecy and expose the truth to her fellow workers—plutonium causes cancer. She blew the whistle on Kerr-McGee's health and safety violations at the Cimarron plant in the vain hope that the AEC would demand better working conditions there, enforce regulations already on its books, and fine the company for each and every regulatory violation. She hoped that a national exposé of quality-control fraud would force the AEC to do its job. Silkwood's ultimate revenge by exposing negligence at the Cimarron plant would be to bring

Kerr-McGee to its corporate knees during contract renewal negotiations and watch it concede major health and safety improvements for her fellow workers.

✦

Snowden didn't want to destroy the NSA. His concern was the nonlethal—but in his view illegal or unconstitutional— invasion of privacy. He accused a secret government organization of using lies and unconstitutional means to protect its citizens from its enemies. He championed the people's right to know what the government was doing in their name.

Silkwood didn't want to destroy Kerr-McGee by getting its Cimarron plant closed. To do so would have been a defeat for OCAW, whose contract with the workers was to save their jobs and improve their working conditions and compensation, not to throw them out of work. She challenged the deceit, corruption, and deadly negligence of the highly protected nuclear industry. She dealt directly with the well-being and potential illness and death of the nuclear workers and their families, as well as the men, women, and children who lived and played near nuclear processing plants that polluted the air they breathed and the water they drank.

But differences aside, Snowden and Silkwood had an important thing in common. They both kicked the hornets' nest. The stings were not far behind.

8

THE PRICE
Snowden

Edward Snowden blew the whistle on the NSA with his ears wide open. He knew with certainty that revealing top-secret government documents came with a price. Like democracy itself, the truth is hardly ever free. If he remained in the United States after he was identified, Snowden knew he would be arrested, tried, and eventually convicted like Wiki leaker Chelsea (formerly Bradley) Manning, who was sentenced to thirty-five years in prison.

To guardians of the Fourth Amendment like Laura Poitras and Glenn Greenwald, the U.S. government seemed all too eager to go after whistleblowers. As Greenwald pointed out: "The Obama administration has prosecuted more government leakers—a total of seven—under the Espionage Act of 1917, than all previous administrations in U.S. history *combined*—in fact, more than double that total."

There was also little doubt in Snowden's mind that, given the national and international ramifications of his leaks, the Justice Department could ask for the death penalty or a life sentence. If Snowden was lucky, he would get jail time like Manning, with the possibility of parole in eight or ten years. There was no chance he'd be treated like William Binney, who blew the whistle on the NSA to Congress and the Department of Justice (among others) in 2002, eleven years before Snowden's revelations.

✦

William Binney was NSA's technical leader for intelligence and the agency's best analyst at the time he resigned in 2001, after more than thirty years of service. He blew the whistle on the NSA for wasting hundreds of millions of dollars on Trailblazer, an ineffective intelligence-gathering program. Trailblazer was poorly designed: it failed to detect plans for 9/11 in advance of the attack. The alternative, far superior program, Thin Thread—developed by Binney and his colleagues—had a filter that would have blocked "intelligence spam," allowing analysts to more easily detect clues and connect the dots. Binney believed that Thin Thread would have thwarted 9/11. His opinion that the NSA had failed to prevent the most devastating terrorist attack on America caused more than just irritation. It certainly didn't endear William Binney to his former NSA bosses.

Binney also blew the whistle on StellarWind, an illegal and unconstitutional NSA program that engaged in warrantless eavesdropping on Americans. Binney estimated that StellarWind had retrieved, among other data, more than a trillion phone calls and e-mails. To cover its tracks and deceive Congress, the NSA hid the illegal program behind the title "Terrorist Surveillance Program."

The big difference between Snowden and Binney is that the Justice Department never charged Binney with a crime; it had no proof that he stole classified NSA documents and delivered them to the media. On the contrary, the Justice Department found Binney's information so valuable that it granted immunity to him and his fellow whistleblower, J. Kirk Wieb. That doesn't mean that Binney didn't pay a price for blowing the whistle on the NSA. He endured years of harassment by the agency, which resulted in serious financial losses that led to the demise of his business and the destruction of his career. (Binney is featured in Laura Poitras's 2014 documentary *Citizenfour*. An interview with him is available on YouTube.)

✦

It's possible that time will prove Snowden was right—that the NSA had indeed violated the U.S. Constitution and/ or acted illegally. In that case, public and congressional sentiment against Snowden might soften, and a future president might commute a sentence to time served. But even if the courts were to eventually rule that the NSA programs Snowden made public were unconstitutional or illegal, Snowden realized that a full pardon would be impossible. He knowingly and willfully violated the Espionage Act of 1917. A full pardon would be viewed as an acknowledgment that the law is cloudy, defective, or unjust. The law is a proud creature that hates to admit it could possibly be wrong or that an apology might be in order.

Snowden understood that once the shriek of his whistle was heard around the world, life as he knew it would be over. He accepted this as the price he would have to pay to reveal classified national security documents. He'd certainly lose his job, a promising and lucrative career, and the support of his family, not to mention his country. Whistleblowing would cost Edward Snowden his freedom—and who knew—one day maybe even his life.

"I understand that I will be made to suffer for my actions," he told Greenwald. "I'm not afraid of what will happen to me. I've accepted that my life will likely be over from my doing this. I'm at peace with that."

Snowden also understood that to survive he would have to seek the fickle protection of a foreign country. Like Salman Rushdie, he would be a hunted man with a yellow Day-Glo target on his back. Furthermore, he knew that if no country was willing to give him asylum, he might be assassinated. Based on the logic of the U.S. war on terror, blowing the whistle on the NSA during wartime is a treasonable act. The traditional punishment for traitors in wartime is death. Therefore, to assassinate Edward Snowden would not only be justified, it would be considered an act of patriotism.

Snowden not only knew this but discussed it openly, calmly, and rationally in his videotaped interviews. Snowden chose to blow the whistle on the NSA and was willing to face the consequences of his revelations, with or without the support of his fellow Americans.

✦

On June 22, 2013, about two weeks after the first Greenwald *Guardian* article appeared online and in print, the Department of Justice charged Edward Snowden with stealing classified documents in violation of the Espionage Act of

1917. Specifically, Attorney General Eric Holder charged Snowden under the Act with "unauthorized communication of national defense information [and] willful communication of classified communications intelligence information to an unauthorized person." None of the charges carried a possible death penalty. Holder declined to charge Snowden with aiding the enemy, which could carry that penalty.

Even so, Snowden calls his own assassination a distinct possibility. "Government officials want to kill me," he said in an interview that was broadcast in Germany in January 2014. Snowden's accusation was based on anonymous online threats like the following that were posted on Buzzfeed.com:

A former Special Forces officer: "I would love to put a bullet in his head. I do not take pleasure in taking another human being's life, having to do it in uniform, but he is single-handedly the greatest traitor in American history."

A defense contractor working at an overseas U.S. intelligence-gathering base: "His name is cursed every day over here. Most everyone I talk to says he needs to be tried and hung . . . forget the trial and just hang him."

A U.S. intelligence officer: "We could end this very quickly. Just casually walking down the streets of Moscow, coming from buying groceries, going back to his flat. He is casually poked by a passerby. He thinks nothing of it at the time, starts to feel a little woozy and thinks it's a parasite from the local water. He goes home very innocently and the next thing you know he dies in the shower."

An NSA analyst: "In a world where I would not be restricted from killing an American, I personally would go and kill him myself. A lot of people share this sentiment."

9

THE PRICE

Silkwood

Like Edward Snowden, Karen Silkwood took on the most powerful government agency of her time, as well as the nuclear industry it supported. But unlike Snowden she lacked both the experience and clarity of vision to guide her choices. Judging from her surprise at the whistleblower backlash she suffered during the last four months of her life, she didn't understand the danger that encircled her like an ever-tightening garrote. Nor did she seem to know whom, other than Kerr-McGee, she ought to fear.

In September 1974, Silkwood stepped into the AEC lair in the nation's capital and exposed the corruption in the commission's Chicago regional office. She could not have known at the time that she was under surveillance as a nuclear terrorist, and had been for nearly two years.

---

*See my book *Useful Enemies: America's Open-Door Policy for Nazi War Criminals* (New York: Delphinium Books, 2013).

✦

From its creation in 1946 to its demise in 1975, the Atomic Energy Commission was the nation's most beloved Cold War behemoth. War isn't about soldiers and armies. It's about soldiers and armies *with weapons*. The AEC had total control over the plutonium and enriched uranium the military needed to maintain and expand its store of weapons and protect the country against nuclear terrorists and nuclear attack. Until its demise, the AEC was so powerful that whatever it wanted, it got. It was a Goliath, backed by Fort Knox, protected by friends on Capitol Hill, supported by the White House, and assisted by the FBI, the CIA, and an ever-expanding NSA. Its hubris was as big as the Washington Monument.

Out of Cold War fear, the U.S. Congress created the AEC under the Atomic Energy Act of 1946. Out of that same fear, the post–World War II military-intelligence complex—with the approval of the Truman White House and the departments of War, State, and Justice—had approved top-secret plans to employ thousands of former Nazis and their collaborators as scientists, spies, consultants, propagandists, and saboteurs.* The United States entered the Vietnam War because it feared the domino effect of communism. The White House approved top-secret NSA programs to invade the phone and Internet privacy of Americans (and others) out of the fear that gave birth to the war on terror.

Congress became harnessed to a set of contradictory missions: provide the plutonium and enriched uranium that the military needed to maintain and expand its nuclear weapons programs; promote the peaceful use of nuclear power; protect the United States from real or suspected nuclear terrorists and their organizations; and, at the same time, protect nuclear workers, their families, the public, and the environment from harmful or deadly radiation. The AEC failed so miserably that Congress was devising a plan to dissolve it even as Karen Silkwood was ticking off to an AEC panel in Bethesda, Maryland, a list of health and safety violations that the commission's regional office in Chicago had swept under the rug it shared with Kerr-McGee.

Under pressure from its constituents, Congress would eventually recognize that the AEC was riven by conflicts of interest and was dangerously secretive, out of control, and out of date. The commission and the military and private nuclear industry it both relied on and promoted were "rotten" to the core. Legislators finally dissolved the AEC in October 1975, eleven months after Karen Silkwood was killed.

✦

To meet congressional mandates, the AEC created a National Laboratory system staffed by handpicked nuclear scientists who had agreed to create and promote deceptive radiation standards—the so-called safe limits and lifetime body limits—to prevent workers' fears and public panic. If Silkwood and the OCAW kept speaking out about gross negligence, how long would it be before they would spark a national debate with non-AEC nuclear scientists who were already challenging the commission's scientists over AEC "safe" limits? It would not be in the interest of winning the Cold War to allow or encourage such a debate at a time when the ranks of antinuclear activists were beginning to swell. Their voice had grown from a whisper to a shout resounding up and down the hallways of Washington at a time when the commission was under the microscope.

Just as important, Silkwood was about to call national attention to Kerr-McGee's faulty fuel rods and the gross negligence at its Cimarron plant. That negligence had resulted in daily contaminations; holes in safety gloves; safety alarms that didn't work or were deliberately disconnected; fraudulent AEC inspections; the use of defective respirators for hours and days; and constantly leaking overhead pipes that carried radioactive liquid that dripped on the workers standing beneath them.

What the OCAW knew in 1974, but Silkwood did not, was that conditions at other AEC-controlled nuclear processing plants, such as those at Oak Ridge, Tennessee, and Apollo, Pennsylvania (to name just two), were just as bad, if not worse, than conditions at Crescent, Oklahoma. A national exposé in the *New York Times* was bound to send shivers through the entire nuclear industry at the height of the Cold War. And it might jeopardize the timely and cost-effective development and delivery of the enriched uranium and plutonium that fed the U.S. nuclear arsenal. It would also fan the flames of the growing antinuclear movement.

✦

What Karen Silkwood also didn't know in 1974 was that the AEC was privy to investigative reports on antinuclear organizations and individuals suspected of nuclear terrorism. As she sat at the AEC conference room table in Bethesda, she didn't know that there was a secret national organization, the Law Enforcement Intelligence Unit (LEIU), that, in the 1970s, specialized in spying on antinuclear organizations and on real or suspected nuclear terrorists like Karen Silkwood.

According to two exposés published soon after Silkwood's death, LEIU was a loose federation of more than 250 U.S. and Canadian law enforcement organizations, mostly police departments and state bureaus of investigation. Founded in 1956 out of frustration with the FBI's refusal to share information with "real" cops, LEIU's stated goal was to track organized crime. By the 1970s, it had a second mission—identify and spy on nuclear terrorists.

As a private vigilante organization or secret police force, LEIU kept dossiers on suspects, which it shared with LEIU members and probably, either directly or indirectly, with the CIA and the NSA. The Law Enforcement Intelligence Unit depended on undercover police detectives to spy on individuals and to penetrate antinuclear organizations. Wiretapping was one of its primary tools.

"The most common type of criminality among LEIU intelligence squads," investigative writer George O'Toole explained in his 1976 exposé, "is illegal wiretapping, which almost always is done with some degree of cooperation from local telephone companies." O'Toole was not suggesting that the CEOs of the telephone companies he named in his story— Chesapeake and Potomac and Southwestern Bell—were necessarily working with LEIU. The secret organization in fact relied on the assistance of telephone operators and linemen. It also recruited informants from hotels, airlines, banks, and other companies. (LEIU has steadfastly denied the warrantless-wiretapping allegations of O'Toole and others.)

Supported in part by secret government funding and a

grant from the Federal Law Enforcement Assistance Administration, LEIU eventually computerized its files, which became the Interstate Organized Crime Index. Besides biographical data and photographs, the index listed the names of friends of the subjects and the organizations they belonged to. To be placed on the suspect list of nuclear terrorists required no actual proof of a crime committed. Any individual LEIU law-enforcement agent could open a file on anyone at any time as long as three or more other LEIU units endorsed the nomination.

LEIU is important to the Silkwood story because the Oklahoma State Bureau of Investigation (OSBI) and the Oklahoma City Police Department had been identified as LEIU members. Both had targeted Karen Silkwood. OSBI admitted under a Freedom of Information Act (FOIA) request that it had investigative reports on Karen Gay Silkwood, but claimed that those files were exempt from disclosure under Oklahoma sunshine laws. Court action against OSBI to release its investigative files on a deceased target like Silkwood would be futile. The Oklahoma state exemption clause has already been challenged in a civil lawsuit asking the court to compel OSBI to release its files on a deceased person. The plaintiff lost. Disclosure was denied. OSBI has not responded to a request for more information on the lawsuit.

◆

Finally, Karen Silkwood didn't know (and couldn't possibly have known in 1974) that the AEC was so powerful and secretive that it had commissioned and funded forty years of radiation experiments on unwitting men, women, and children. The General Accountability Office (GAO) reported that it had identified over 210,000 radiation test participants. The report went on to say that precise numbers were not, and never will be, available. Americans did not learn about the experiments until the 1990s, nearly twenty years after Silkwood's death and after the collapse of the Soviet Union and the end of the Cold War. Those unethical and probably criminal experiments demonstrated the airtight secrecy of the AEC, its vast financial resources, the depth and scope of its Cold War pragmatism, its lack of respect for human life, and its fundamental inhumanity. The record speaks for itself.

The purpose of the AEC's experiments on humans was to harm or eventually kill the subjects by feeding them, injecting into them, or otherwise exposing them to excessive levels of radiation in order to study their effects on the human body. Perhaps the most brutal example of the inhumanity of the experiments was the feeding of radiated oatmeal to a group of mentally challenged orphans, according to the GAO.

As part of its 1994 hearings, the staff of the U.S. House of Representatives Subcommittee on Administrative Law and Governmental Relations compiled a fifty-page summary of the radiation experiments titled *Government-Sponsored Testimony on Humans*. The AEC-sponsored experiments listed in that summary included the following:

- Between 1961 and 1965, the Massachusetts Institute of Technology (MIT) fed radium and thorium to twenty men and women, ages sixty-three to eighty-three, who resided at a Boston area home for the elderly. The purpose of the experiment was to determine how much radiation the body retained and how quickly the body eliminated it. MIT and the AEC told the volunteer subjects that they would be participating in a study on aging.

- Between 1953 and 1957, approximately twenty patients at Massachusetts General Hospital in Boston—all terminally ill with brain tumors—were unknowingly injected with uranium to determine the dose at which kidney damage would occur.

- Between 1963 and 1965, the AEC's Idaho National Laboratory, located in an isolated, eastern part of the state, deliberately released radioactive iodine over neighboring farmlands. Then it fed unwitting subjects radioactive milk produced by cows that had grazed on the contaminated grass. The purpose of the experiment was to trace the passage of the iodine through the food chain and into the thyroid of the human subjects.

- Between 1961 and 1963, the University of Chicago and the AEC's Argonne National Laboratory fed 102 human subjects disguised nuclear fallout from the Nevada test site. The purpose was to measure the rate and degree of radiation absorption into the body.

- In 1963, Battelle Memorial Institute in Richland, Washington, fed five subjects fish from the Columbia River. The fish were contaminated with radioactive substances produced and discarded into the river by nuclear reactors at the nearby AEC Hanford site called the Reservation. (Ten years later, Silkwood uncovered defective fuel rods destined for the same site.)

One follow-up study of eighteen patients injected with plutonium, cited by the House subcommittee, reported that nine patients had died within three years; one had died within eight years; one lasted eleven years and one fourteen; four lasted twenty years. Only one was still alive after twenty years. One could not be found.

✦

What Karen Silkwood did know in the fall of 1974 was that up to forty pounds of plutonium was missing from the Cimarron plant. That plutonium—euphemistically called material unaccounted for (MUF)—was no secret to the Cimarron plant workers. Kerr-McGee managers had been checking and rechecking their plutonium bookkeeping records, shelves, desk drawers, and nooks and crannies for months. They never found it. Neither did the FBI. The Bureau had been investigating the MUF since 1974, the year Silkwood was killed, according to FBI records recently obtained under an FOIA request.

What made Karen Silkwood's discovery special was that she had stumbled on the actual amount missing—enough to make four atomic/nuclear bombs. That specificity indicated that she had seen the AEC-mandated plutonium inventory reports. Several weeks before she died—while she was under great pressure and very frightened—Silkwood phoned a fellow lab worker and told him about the forty pounds of MUF. He would testify at the 1979 negligence trial against Kerr-McGee instigated by the Silkwood family that not only had Silkwood called him about the missing plutonium but he had made a note of the call and its content in his diary, which he shared with the judge and jury.

MUF figures and locations were classified in 1974 and still are today. Were the Cimarron plant inventory reports revealing the MUF figure among the documents that Silkwood had collected and planned to deliver to the *New York Times*? Was she a woman who knew too much?

✦

Without doubt, Karen Silkwood was considered to be a dangerous woman who faced off with the Kerr-McGee Nuclear Corporation, one of the largest energy conglomerates in the country; the negligent and corrupt AEC's Chicago regional office; and the AEC national leadership, which looked the other way and cozied up to its nuclear subcontractors. In effect, Silkwood challenged the image, power, and secrecy of the AEC. What she was about to do in Crescent for the OCAW and the *New York Times* would not be glad tidings to the beleaguered commission, which was already under attack from the Congress that created and nurtured it. And she indirectly challenged the FBI, LEIU, OSBI, CIA, NSA, and the Oklahoma City Police—all of whom kept a close eye on the Cimarron plant. To them, Karen Silkwood was easy prey—a starling sitting on a fence post in rural Oklahoma.

10

SILKWOOD
Death

After returning to work at the Cimarron plant, Karen Silkwood and Local 5-283 leader Jack Tice were formally reprimanded for campaigning against the decertification vote
during their coffee and lunch breaks. Kerr-McGee argued
that the breaks were "company time" and, by contract,
union reps were forbidden to conduct union business on
company time. Tice called the National Labor Relations
Board (NLRB) for a ruling.

Kerr-McGee was a sore loser.

In a sworn deposition taken three years after Silkwood's
death, James Smith, formerly divisional manager at the Cimarron plant, described the "punishment" meted out to
union leaders. Smith had more than twenty years of experience working with AEC-controlled plutonium, first at
Rocky Flats, Colorado, then at Crescent. He was deeply
troubled by what he saw at the Kerr-McGee plant in the
fall of 1974, two months before Silkwood died. Almost
every OCAW antidecertification campaigner, Smith testi-

fied, ended up on the "rock pile," supervised by a foreman whose only job was to never let them out of his sight. "They pulled them all off the process area and put them out there to sweeping sidewalks," Smith testified. "[They] had a guard with them all the time like a bunch of convict labor."

It was easy for the plant manager to spot union troublemakers. He had spies everywhere and always seemed to know what the union was planning. "[He] would come to the management meeting in the morning," Smith testified, "and mention something that had taken place at or . . . [was] said at the meeting."

Smith went on to testify that, based on reports from his informants, the plant manager would give his supervisors a list of workers to be sent to the rock pile. The idea was to isolate them so they couldn't talk freely to their fellow workers. Almost everyone who played a role in the union antidecertification campaign made the list.

Jack Tice got the worst treatment. The plant manager assigned him to do janitorial work in the neighboring nonunion uranium factory built in 1970, two years before the plutonium plant opened for business. "That place wasn't fit for man or beast," Smith testified. "You never saw such a pigpen in your life. . . . Uranium everywhere. You could wade in it, go by and see piles of it on the floor. . . . You could look at it on the people's clothes . . . powder, black smudges, green smudges." And since Kerr-McGee and the AEC didn't require its uranium workers to wear protective booties, they brought the contamination home with them.

Although Karen Silkwood never ended up on the rock pile, she felt the lash of Kerr-McGee. First, the plant manager separated Silkwood and fellow union rep Jerry Brewer, who worked with her in the lab, so they couldn't communicate with or support each other. He transferred Brewer from the tidy lab to a dirty job in a warehouse. Then the plant manager ordered Silkwood's boss to "give her a bad time." The lab supervisor refused. "I don't give a damn what they say about her," he told Smith. "She's still a good tech, and she does her job, and she doesn't give me any trouble."

Blocked by Silkwood's supervisor, the plant manager changed tactics. He trimmed the lab staff just as Kerr-McGee increased production quotas. That meant less quality control and more work for Silkwood. She ended up doing the pellet and rod inspections normally performed by two or more technicians. But despite the stress of an increased workload, Silkwood continued to follow up on the ever-increasing—and predictable—contaminations. She got little or no co-operation from the plant manager and supervisors. Health physics director Wayne Norwood even tried to prevent her from checking on the condition of workers who were being nose-swiped, probed, urine-sampled, and scrubbed in the health physics office.

"You have no right to be here," Norwood threatened.

Silkwood refused to be intimidated. As a union rep responsible for health and safety, she argued, it was her duty to observe and report. If Norwood wanted to file an official complaint, he was welcome to, but until either her union boss or the NLRB told her not to, she would continue to come to the health physics office and review the level of worker contamination and what—if anything—Kerr-McGee was doing about it.

✦

Pressure continued to mount all through October and into November, both before and after the local beat the decertification vote. To some extent, the backlash was Silkwood's own fault. Before her secret visit to Washington, she was concerned about worker health and safety. After the trip, she became passionate and driven. The union and her mission became the center of her life. After finishing her ten-hour shift, she would stay late in the Metallography Laboratory to pore over quality-control records. As Mazzocchi had instructed, she made sure that what she was doing appeared to be part of her job. She studied X-rays of rod welds and discovered that someone was touching them up with a felt-tipped pen to hide defects. She discovered data in the quality-control reports manipulated to hide the fact that defective rods, some with defective plutonium pellets, were being shipped to the AEC fast-flux nuclear reactor at Hanford, Washington.

Silkwood also reviewed X-rays of randomly selected pellets that had passed line inspection. She found more and more defective because plant management had speeded up pellet production from one lot per week to four lots per week. If workers weren't deliberately cutting corners to meet their quotas, they were so exhausted by working ten to twelve hours a day, sometimes wearing uncomfortable respirators, that they missed what would be more obvious under better working conditions.

"They're still passing high welds no matter what the picture looks like," Silkwood reported in a phone call to Steve Wodka two weeks after she returned from Washington. "We grind down too far and I got a weld I would love for you to see—just how far they ground it down till we lost the weld, trying to get rid of the voids and inclusions and cracks."

Motivated by typical antiwhistleblower fear and resentment, most workers at the Cimarron plant (union and nonunion alike) failed to appreciate that Silkwood was trying to improve their health and safety. They began to harass her. First they shunned, then attacked her. *You're rocking the boat. You're just making things worse by picking on Kerr-McGee. You're taking our jobs away. You're going to get the plant shut down. You're a bitch.*

The harassment went beyond shunning and name calling. Karen Silkwood sensed that she was being followed, but she couldn't prove it. Noticing the way her belongings had been rearranged, she knew that her work locker and car had been searched more than once. She suspected that someone was looking for the documents she had stolen from the company—in effect from the AEC—but she couldn't prove it.

Silkwood's roommate, Sherri Ellis, a nonunion lab technician who worked a different ten-hour shift than Silkwood, used to leave their apartment door unlocked when she left for work. Silkwood suspected that someone had searched her home after Ellis left and before she returned. Silkwood was worried enough to check her hiding place behind a removable ceiling panel in her bedroom closet to make sure her evidence was still there.

Was she suffering from typical whistleblower paranoia? Or was she really being spied on, followed, and searched? If so, by whom? Kerr-McGee security personnel? The FBI? The Oklahoma City police intelligence officers? Freelancers hired by the AEC? And more important, was her apartment phone bugged?

♦

After Silkwood's death and in preparation for their civil suit against Kerr-McGee, the Silkwood family's investigators would begin an undercover search for wiretapping evidence. Bill Taylor, a former marine with special combat training and with contacts in every segment of the intelligence community, led the investigation. Taylor began his snooping in Fort Lauderdale, home of the most sophisticated wiretapping and spook school in the country—the Audio Intelligence Devices Corporation (AID) and National Intelligence Academy (NIA).

The forces behind AID/NIA were Jack Holcomb and Leo Goodwin Sr. Holcomb described himself as a private detective and freelance wiretapper who had done black-bag jobs for more than four hundred law enforcement agencies, including the FBI. Goodwin was a former paratrooper, Army intelligence officer, and Texas Ranger, and a millionaire police buff. They made an ideal team. Holcomb had the know-how. Goodwin had the bucks. Their school taught law-enforcement and intelligence officers from around the world how to snoop using the most sophisticated bugging equipment available. The school operated out of a highly secured building in Fort Lauderdale. But not secure enough to keep Bill Taylor out.

What Taylor knew before he broke into AID/NIA headquarters was that the school taught intelligence officers from the Oklahoma City Police Department and the Oklahoma Bureau of Investigation, and sold them the equipment they needed back home. Inside the school Taylor saw a fully equipped telephone city with nearly every kind of indoor and outdoor terminal used by U.S. telephone companies. In the middle of the room sat a fully rigged telephone pole, which the students used for practice.

Taylor was salivating at the prospect of meeting Leo Goodwin Jr, who had succeeded his father and inherited his fortune. Taylor thought Goodwin would be less suspicious than Holcomb, a trained sleuth. Under the pretext of wanting to buy some surveillance equipment, Taylor set up a meeting with Goodwin at his home. Two days before the scheduled interview, Goodwin, sixty-three, dropped dead. Taylor managed to procure a copy of the death certificate. He learned that unnamed doctors had performed an autopsy and that the primary cause of death was listed as "congestive heart failure." The doctor who signed the certificate had never viewed the body, making the document suspect. He also refused Taylor's request for an interview. If that wasn't frustrating enough, Jack Holcomb skipped the country when he heard from his former students in Oklahoma that the Silkwood legal team had secured court permission to subpoena him.

While Taylor was sniffing around the intelligence community in Fort Lauderdale, the Silkwood legal team was busy asking the court for more subpoenas. They were especially eager to depose Thomas Bunting, a former Air Force intelligence officer who had joined the Oklahoma State OSBI in 1972, the year Silkwood began working for Kerr-McGee. At the time of Silkwood's death, Bunting was supervisor of the criminal conspiracies unit and taught photographic and electronic surveillance. More likely than not, he had been trained at the Fort Lauderdale school. As supervisor of the very unit that had Silkwood under surveillance, he would know not only what kind of surveillance, but also who had followed her from the Hub Café the night she died and who, if anyone, had forced her off the road.

At first, Bunting tried to duck the subpoena. But after much soul-searching, he had a change of heart. According to his two daughters, Lynn and Debbie, he decided not to fight but to do the right thing. He would answer all the questions Silkwood attorneys put to him, honestly and truthfully. He would not invoke his Fifth Amendment rights or decline to answer a question because it was classified information. Bunting understood that the truth would make him a pariah in the intelligence community—a whistleblower like Karen Silkwood. And knowing firsthand what that intelligence community was capable of, he was worried about retaliation against him and his family.

Before he could be deposed, Bunting, forty-four, walked into his brother's home and passed out as Leo Goodwin did in Fort Lauderdale. He was rushed to the hospital, where he was pronounced dead. As with Leo Goodwin, a doctor ruled that Bunting had died of a heart attack, apparently induced by a cerebral hemorrhage. Bunting had not been ill, and a recent physical examination had not revealed a heart condition. Bunting's wife, Sue, declined to request an autopsy. His first wife, who found her former husband's death highly suspicious, had begged for one.

Not long before his death, Thomas Bunting had revised his insurance policy, making Sue his sole beneficiary. She inherited all his assets, including his police death benefits. Several months after her husband's death, Sue Bunting was found dead in her car, which was parked in the garage with the motor running. Her blood alcohol was extremely high. Her death was ruled a suicide. Thomas Bunting's daughters didn't buy it. They believed that their father was murdered. Was Sue Bunting a co-conspirator in the death of their father? Did someone, in turn, murder her because she was attempting to blackmail her fellow conspirator(s)? When one of the daughters asked several OCPD officers who knew her father what had really happened, they told her that they couldn't talk about the Karen Silkwood case. If they did, they would be fired.

If there was any doubt that the intelligence community was capable of murder, it was settled in Fort Lauderdale once and for all. When Bill Taylor returned to his darkened motel room one night, two assassins were waiting. One attacked him with a knife. Using his Marine face-to-face combat training skills, Taylor managed to turn the knife around and stab his assailant. With help from his partner, Taylor's assailant fled through the patio door. Several days later, Taylor found a "John Doe" body in the local morgue. The man had died of a knife wound to the stomach.

Although there was evidence as well as hearsay that OSBI and the OCPD had bugged Silkwood's phone, there was no smoking gun. Several witnesses—some reliable, some not—told investigators that they had seen transcripts of Silkwood's phone calls. And a former police secretary told investigators that one of her jobs was to type the transcripts of Karen Silkwood's telephone calls. Those transcripts are excluded from disclosure under a loophole provision in the Freedom of Information Act and Oklahoma law.

✦

If the phone-tapping and bugging of Karen Silkwood remains unproven, the spying certainly is not. Evidence that the FBI, OSBI, and LEIU had Silkwood under close surveil-

lance is irrefutable. How extensive and invasive the Kerr-
McGee spying was, however, is not known and probably
never will be. What we do know is that Cimarron plant security director James Reading, a retired OCPD intelligence
officer who was cozy with the FBI, hired Steve Campbell,
a cop-friendly photographer, to infiltrate Silkwood's inner
circle. Silkwood's boyfriend Drew Stephens testified in a
sworn deposition that he, Karen, and Campbell spent eve-
nings sitting around her apartment drinking, listening to
music, and shooting the bull. In an attempt to entrap them,
Campbell steered the conversation to Kerr-McGee and nuclear power. He was so cool about it that neither Drew nor
Karen knew he was trying to set them up.

When Campbell learned that Drew was so worried about
Karen that he had begun keeping a diary in case something
happened to her, Campbell filched the notebook and photographed each page before returning it. Then he delivered the
photos to Reading, who paid him $180 (nearly a thousand
dollars in today's dollars). Reading passed the diary photos
on to the FBI in Oklahoma City.

The harassment, rejection, tension, pressure, and spying—real, suspected, or imagined—began to gnaw on Silkwood. She couldn't sleep. She lost weight, dropping from
115 to 94 pounds. As a fellow worker put it, she looked "like
death." Drew tried to get her to quit Kerr-McGee as he had
already in fear for his life and distrust of Kerr-McGee and
the AEC. Drew recognized that the plant and the union
were consuming Karen mentally, spiritually, and physically.
Her doctor prescribed Quaaludes to help her relax and get
some sleep.

Two weeks before the new contract negotiations with

Kerr-McGee were to begin, Silkwood called her mother, Merle, and begged her to send job applications for the oil companies around Nederland, Texas, her parents' hometown. She said she was thinking of quitting Kerr-McGee and coming home. But not until her union work at the Cimarron plant was finished.

Silkwood also called her sister Rosemary. Through gulps and sobs, she managed to say that someone was trying to do something to her. That something was happening to her. She was afraid of the plant. She couldn't talk about it. Not over the phone. She said she was quitting. Soon after December 1, when the new Kerr-McGee contract was to be signed.

✦

On Tuesday, November 5, 1974, at 5:30 in the afternoon, Silkwood donned a pair of white overalls, taped lightweight plastic gloves to her wrists, and began to grind, clean, and polish plutonium pellets inside a sealed box. She handled the pellets with thick rubber gloves over the plastic gloves that reached from her fingertips to her shoulders. An hour later, she slipped out of the gloves in box no. 3 and checked both hands on a monitor. It began clicking.

A health technician monitored her clothes and exposed skin for radiation. Her left hand, right wrist, upper arm, neck, face, and hair were all hot. The worst reading was on her right wrist, which read twenty times over the limit deemed safe by the AEC. Next, the technician took nasal smears. Both nostrils registered positive and high. Meanwhile, another technician in a respirator monitored the air in the lab. The room and its filter were clean. Then he poured water into the sealed gloves Silkwood had used. They didn't leak, but the outsides were contaminated by insoluble plutonium. The radiation defied physics and logic. How did insoluble plutonium get on the gloves? Nothing else in the room was hot. No one knew. Just as no one knew how Silkwood had been contaminated nine weeks earlier, on July 31.

After showering and scrubbing her skin with a blend of Clorox and Tide to remove surface contamination, Silkwood went to her lab office to work on the quality-control paperwork piled on her desk. Then she went into the darkroom next to the lab to develop the pellet inspection film. At one o'clock in the morning, she locked the lab door, picked up her urine and fecal specimen kits, monitored herself—she was clean—and went home to get some sleep.

It had been another twelve-hour day at Kerr-McGee. The long-awaited union-management negotiations were to open in the morning. Silkwood's presence at the meeting was important to the union and the future of the Kerr-Mc-Gee workers. No one knew more about health and safety violations at the Cimarron plant than Karen Silkwood.

Having caught only a few hours of sleep, on the morning of November 6 Silkwood arrived at the plutonium plant a few minutes before eight. It promised to be an exhausting day. Contract negotiations were scheduled for nine o'clock in the conference room at the uranium plant next door. Silkwood had managed to catch only a few hours of sleep and knew she was facing an exhausting day. She did paperwork in her lab office for an hour, then monitored herself for radiation before leaving the plant. Her right forearm was hot—ten times over the limit deemed safe by the AEC. Soap and water didn't wash it away. Even worse, her nasal readings

that morning were higher than they had been the day before. She was so hot that she was afraid she would be barred
from attending the negotiations. Health physics director
Wayne Norwood, who had next to no academic training in
the health physics field, told her not to worry. The contamination was embedded so deeply in her skin that she posed
no danger to others.

How was Karen Silkwood contaminated when she was
in the plutonium plant for only an hour? And only in her
lab office? For the third time, no one knew. If the intention
was to stop Silkwood from entering the plant or attending
the union-management negotiation, it almost succeeded.
She spent the day in a state of panic, while sparring with
Kerr-McGee negotiators. That night Silkwood called Pro-
fessor Abrahamson in Minnesota. She was crying. She was
afraid of dying of cancer, she told him.

Silkwood returned to the plutonium plant just before
eight the following morning. She brought her specimen
kits, urine and fecal samples, with her. Norwood was now
nearly as worried as Silkwood. If she was hot, he didn't want
her to contaminate other workers. He insisted on taking another nasal smear before allowing her to enter the work area
of the plant. Both nostrils—even the one that was partially
blocked due to a childhood accident—read extremely high.
Norwood then placed a specially designed radiation monitor
against her fecal kit. It also read very high. The fecal contamination suggested that Silkwood might have eaten insoluble plutonium. Norwood would not allow her to remain
inside the plant.

The sequence of events made it clear to Norwood that
Silkwood's contamination on both mornings *had not* orig-

inated at the plant. That left Silkwood's locker, car, and apartment. The locker and car were clean. By contrast, the apartment was so hot that health physics technicians donned full-face respirators, special galoshes, and gloves taped to their white coveralls before they began tossing the contents of the apartment into fifty-five-gallon metal drums lined with plastic. The barrels would later be buried in a dump. It didn't take Norwood long to figure out how both Karen Silkwood and her apartment had been contaminated. Lab records showed that someone had been spiking her urine kits with insoluble plutonium ever since she returned from her Washington trip. And she had spilt some of the contaminated urine on her bathroom floor before leaving for work that morning. Either the kit had been spiked in the plant, or someone smuggled plutonium into her apartment and spiked it there.

Silkwood's contamination was so severe that the AEC sent her to its Los Alamos, New Mexico, laboratory, which housed the most sophisticated full-body radiation counter in the country. Before she left for New Mexico, she called her mother. She had been contaminated again, she sobbed into the payphone. She was dying. There was no treatment for what she had. She was coming home.

◆

On the morning of November 11, two days before she died, Karen Silkwood stepped into the Los Alamos lab's nine-foot-square radiation counter wearing white paper pajamas and brown paper slippers. Made of seven-inch-thick, pre–World War II battleship steel, the cell looked like a giant bank vault. She sat down in what looked like a dentist's chair. A technician draped her in a light white cotton blanket. A sodium-iodine detector hovered over each breast, counting the amount of plutonium in her lungs.

That afternoon, Silkwood met with Dr. George Voelz, a forty-eight-year-old AEC physician in charge of health services at the Los Alamos laboratory. Dr. Voelz had spent his whole professional life at the site. Beginning as early as 1946, a year after World War II ended and the Cold War began, the AEC had conducted plutonium experiments on unwitting Los Alamos employees. As a resident AEC physician, Dr. Voelz had probably participated in those experiments.

Sitting on the desk in front of Voelz were the results of Silkwood's full-body count. In a cultivated, gentle bedside manner, the doctor reassured her that she had only eight nanocuries of plutonium in her lungs. He explained that the AEC maximum permissible lung burden for plutonium workers was eighteen nanocuries. Her contamination, he pointed out, amounted to less than half the AEC permissible lung burden. After admitting that the full-body radiation counter wasn't perfect—she could have more or less than eight nanocuries of plutonium—Dr. Voelz told Silkwood that she shouldn't have any significant health problems. What if she had babies, Silkwood asked. They should be normal, he told her.

What Dr. Voelz didn't tell Silkwood was that each nanocurie of plutonium emits 2,000 cell-destroying alpha particles every minute for 24,000 years—like an Uzi spitting bullets. Or that most nuclear scientists and physicians—including some working for the AEC—thought the AEC-permissible lung burden of eighteen nanocuries was ridiculously high. Dr. John Gofman, an internationally recognized expert on radiation, would go further during the negligence trial against Kerr-McGee and would testify that AEC permissible body or organ burdens were "an unmitigated lie . . . a legalized permit to murder," and that anyone with as much plutonium in her lungs as Karen Silkwood had was "unequivocally . . . married to cancer."

✦

November 13, the day after Silkwood returned to Crescent from Los Alamos, was the last day of her life. Symbolically, it began and ended with union meetings. In the morning she attended the second contract negotiation at the uranium plant. In the evening she went to a union debriefing meeting for rank-and-file members in the back room of the Hub Café in Crescent. The news was bad. Kerr-McGee was refusing to budge on health and safety demands. Its negotiators argued that the Cimarron plant was losing money, and that it couldn't afford the costly improvements the union was demanding.

Silkwood appeared to be tired but she didn't nod or fall asleep. She drank iced tea. And during a break, she called Drew to make sure that David Burnham of the *New York Times* had arrived and was waiting for her at the Holiday Inn Northwest in Oklahoma City. After the union meeting adjourned around 7:30, Silkwood climbed into her white Honda Civic and headed south out of Crescent down Highway 74 toward Oklahoma City. Minutes and 7.3 miles later, her body lay trapped and crushed inside the Honda in a ditch on the left side of the road. Death was instantaneous.

11

DEMONIZATION

Snowden: Publicity Hound, Coward, Liar

The most powerful gun in the damage-control arsenal isn't truth. It is demonization—a vicious assault on the character of the whistleblower in order to destroy credibility and distract from the message. The damage controller's bag of tricks is as old as Machiavelli.

Find anything that borders on illegal behavior in the whistleblower's past, such as court convictions, messy divorces, arrest reports, domestic violence complaints, a history of alcohol, child support issues, or drug abuse. Attack the whistleblower's motive by alleging that he or she was driven by malice, revenge, deceit, greed, or hunger for publicity. Dig up colleagues, neighbors, and fellow workers who are willing to say, true or untrue, that the whistleblower is vindictive, sneaky, dishonest, prone to exaggerate, not a team player, disruptive in the workplace. Allege that the whistleblower is incompetent at his or her job, cannot be trusted with responsibility, or lacks leadership skills. Accuse the whistleblower of being a thief who stole proprietary documents, illegally revealed company secrets, broke a confidentiality agreement. Label the whistleblower mentally unstable.

Edward Snowden—"the world's most wanted man by the world's most powerful government"—wasn't surprised that his enemies tried to assassinate his character. He expected as much. As he told Greenwald and the *Guardian*, "I know the government will demonize me. They'll say I violated the Espionage Act. That I committed grave crimes. That I aided America's enemies. That I endangered national security. I'm sure they'll grab every incident they can find from my past and probably will exaggerate or even fabricate some to demonize me as much as possible. . . . What keeps a person passive and compliant is fear of repercussions. . . . I decided a while ago that I can live with whatever they do to me. The only thing I can't live with is knowing that I did nothing."

On the one hand, Snowden didn't make it easy for demonizers. His personal life was squeaky clean. No arrest record. No string of parking tickets or DUIs. No fellow workers willing to denigrate his character, and no unsatisfactory work evaluations. No reports of drunken behavior or girlfriend abuse. No drug paraphernalia sitting around his apartment.

On the other hand, Snowden's actions and statements presented his enemies with a lineup of emotionally charged targets carefully chosen to rouse the patriotic instincts of Americans. Edward Snowden is an egocentric publicity hound, a coward, and a liar. He is a spy, a traitor, and a criminal who betrayed his country.

✦

Edward Snowden is an egocentric publicity hound.

The damage controllers are quick to point out that all you have to do is turn on the television or browse YouTube, read the *Guardian,* or scan social media blogs, and you'll find Edward Snowden waiting for you. Snowden's hunger for attention is so great, they claim, that you see him grinning on television shows beamed from Hong Kong, Berlin, Moscow, and London. And don't forget Laura Poitras's Academy Award-winning documentary, *Citizenfour,* featuring Snowden's smirking face. And what about his string of hero awards like Germany's Whistleblower Prize? And the dozens of invitations to deliver telecast speeches like the British annual Alternative Christmas Message. And how about Snowden making the short list for the 2013 Nobel Peace Prize? And don't forget the upcoming Oliver Stone movie *Snowden.* Has Edward Snowden ever turned down an interview request?

Do Snowden's critics make a valid point? In accusing him of being a publicity hound, they are attacking the motive-behind-the-motive and challenging his integrity. Did he lie when he said that his objective was to expose massive and potentially criminal or unconstitutional spying and stimulate open debate? Wasn't his true motive—conscious or subconscious—more personal? Wasn't it to bask in the warmth of the spotlight as a self-proclaimed martyr? To earn a place in history?

Snowden denies the characterization. "I don't want public attention because I don't want the story to be about *me*," he told Glenn Greenwald. "I really want the focus to be on these documents and the debate—which I hope this [document release] will trigger around the globe—about what kind of world we want to live in. . . . My sole motive is to inform the public to that which is done in their name, and that which is done against them."

Snowden makes an important distinction. There are three types of media stories swirling around him—those that deal with his personal life, those that cover his career, and those that focus on his message. He welcomes all the message attention he can get, while claiming he doesn't want the personal attention and merely tolerates the spotlight on his professional career. "Unfortunately, the mainstream media now seem far more interested in what I said when I was seventeen," he complained in a live chat with *Guardian* readers. "Or what my girlfriend looks like, rather than, say, the largest program of suspicionless surveillance in human history."

But Snowden can't have it both ways. The minute he faced Poitras's video camera in his hotel room in Hong Kong and revealed himself as the source of the NSA stories published in the *Guardian* and the *Washington Post,* he opened the door to his personal and professional life. In effect, by identifying himself as the leaker, Snowden made half of his story *about me.*

The canon of media questions is deceptively simple. Before it asks what, when, where, why, and how, it asks *who.* In Snowden's case, the answer to *who* does more than just satisfy curiosity or pander to prurient interests. It lays a foundation for motive, which, next to truth, is the most critical element in evaluating the whistleblower. *Who* explores the whistleblower's professional credentials, and these are important to establishing credibility.

Snowden supporters point out that his eagerness to explain to the media what his documents reveal and why he decided to leak them should come as no surprise. They say he has been consistent in stating his basic motive—to tell the world what the U.S. government is doing so that the people can exercise their right to decide whether they want the government to spy on them. One can hardly "tell the world" without using the media to the fullest extent.

✦

Edward Snowden is a coward.

Snowden's enemies and critics are eager to point out that he fled the United States to avoid arrest and punishment and that he is hiding in foreign countries instead of manning up to the charges against him. They say that makes him a coward. Such an allegation strikes a deep chord in the soul of Americans who consider themselves patriotic and want to believe that turning himself in would be the honorable thing to do.

From his hotel room in Hong Kong, Snowden argued his defense: "I am not planning to hide who and what I am so I have no reason to go into hiding and feed conspiracy theories or demonizing comparisons. . . . I am not here to hide from justice. I'm here to reveal criminality."

A coward is a person who lacks the courage to do, or endure, dangerous or unpleasant things. Does Snowden lack the courage to return to the United States to face the three criminal counts against him—theft of classified documents, possession of classified documents, and giving those classified documents to unauthorized people. If he returns and is convicted, he could get life in prison.

Snowden has repeatedly said that he is willing to return

to the United States to face a judge and jury, and that if he does, there would be "a huge chance" that he would go to prison. He's willing to take that risk, he says, as long as he is guaranteed his constitutional right to a fair trial. He argues that the government is not offering him a fair trial for several reasons.

The government has publicly declared him guilty rather than innocent until proven guilty. And it has defined "the disclosure of secret, criminal—and even unconstitutional acts—as an unforgiveable crime." But whether or not the disclosure is an unforgiveable crime is for a jury to decide, not the government.

To prevent classified information from being revealed in a public trial and to deny Snowden a propaganda platform, the Justice Department planned to try Snowden in a closed court under the provisions of the Classified Information Procedures Act. Passed by Congress in 1980, the act's primary function is to prevent criminal defendants from blackmailing the government—or "graymailing," as it is frequently called. The defendant presents the Justice Department with an either-or proposition—dismiss the charges or I will disclose classified information in my defense. Snowden argues that a closed court trial is a denial of his constitutional rights.

Finally, the Justice Department demands that Snowden plead guilty before it will negotiate terms for his return to the U.S. Snowden refuses to do so. He is willing to admit that he violated the provisions of the Espionage Act of 1917, but he is unwilling to concede that he committed a crime in doing so.

In demanding and defining the terms of a fair trial, Snowden is again being consistent. Wearing a muzzle is not an option. He has said over and over that he wants to tell Americans how the government is spying on them so that they can decide for themselves if they want to pay that price for protection in the era of the war on terror.

Snowden's supporters point out that he declined to blow the whistle anonymously because he didn't want innocent people to be hounded by government agents. Unlike most of the character assassins, who choose to work in the shadows and accuse him anonymously, Snowden faced Laura Poitras's unforgiving camera. "I believe I have an obligation to explain why I'm doing this and what I hope to achieve," he said. "I'm not afraid of what will happen to me. . . . I know it's the right thing to do."

In the opening credits of Poitras's film, *Citizenfour,* the screen freezes on the words "NSA Whistleblower." Then Snowden appears and says calmly, but with an anxiety that the viewer can feel rather than see: "My name is Ed Snowden. I'm twenty-nine years old. I worked for Booz Allen Hamilton as an infrastructure analyst for NSA in Hawaii."

Is that cowardice? Snowden supporters ask his anonymous character assassins.

◆

Edward Snowden is a liar.

Snowden said that he reported his concerns about the legality of NSA's spy programs to his superiors. His detractors say that is a lie. Furthermore, they note that while he rails against America as an Orwellian state, he chose to hide in Russia, an Orwellian state. That, they say, makes him a hypocrite.

In sworn testimony before the European parliament, Snowden said that he had voiced his concerns about what he considered to be illegal NSA spy programs to at least ten NSA officials. He was more specific in interviews with *NBC Nightly News* and the *Washington Post.* "The NSA has records," he told NBC. "They have copies of e-mails right now to their Office of General Counsel, to their oversight and compliance folks—from me—raising concerns about the NSA's interpretation of its legal authorities."

In an exclusive interview with *Post* reporters, Snowden said that he had raised his concerns about NSA spy programs to two superiors in NSA's Technology Directorate and to two in the Agency's Threat Operations Center in Hawaii. Consistent with his concern about shielding the identities of intelligence personnel, Snowden declined to reveal the names of the officials to whom he complained or to make public his e-mails to them.

In response to Snowden's claims, NSA officials who spoke on condition of anonymity told the *Washington Post* that "after extensive investigation, including interviews with his former supervisors and coworkers, we have not found any evidence to support Mr. Snowden's contention that he brought these matters to anyone's attention." NSA deputy director Rick Ledgett, who spoke on the record, dodged the issue with a lawyerly sidestep. He said that Snowden made no *formal* complaints. Then he conveniently neglected to define the word "formal." Except for its deceptive premise, Ledgett's straw man logic was airtight: For a complaint to be recognized as a complaint, it must be formal.

Snowden did not issue a formal complaint.

Therefore, Snowden did not issue a complaint.

Ledgett went on to say that if Snowden complained personally or informally, no one has come forward to acknowledge it.

In response to Ledgett and the anonymous NSA officials, Snowden threw down the gauntlet. "I directly challenge the NSA to deny that I contacted NSA oversight and compliance bodies directly via e-mail," he said, "and that I specifically expressed concerns about their suspect interpretation of the law. And I welcome members of Congress to request a written answer to this question."

The issue is basically a high-stakes, he said-they said spat. Who is telling the truth? Who is bending the truth? Who is lying? Snowden supporters argue that the NSA and the intelligence community are the liars, not Edward Snowden. The existence of NSA programs like PRISM and BOUNDLESS INFORMANT prove, they point out, that NSA officials have been lying to Congress for years about the scope and breadth of the agency's bulk spying on Americans. Defenders of Snowden also point out that both NSA director General Keith B. Alexander and National Intelligence director James Clapper lied to Congress about NSA programs. (Lying to Congress is a felony.) *Citizenfour* contains bone-chilling clips of their false sworn testimony.

In one clip, Senator Ron Wyden, an Oregon Democrat, asks Clapper: "Does the NSA collect any type of data at all on millions of Americans?"

"No, sir," Clapper testifies without blinking an eye.

"It does not?" Wyden asks.

"Not wittingly," Clapper replies.

In light of NSA's long history of deceit, and in response

to accusations that Edward Snowden lied, his supporters ask: Why should the public believe *anything* the NSA says unless it presents compelling evidence that leaves no doubt? Or to put their concern another way—one should assume that the NSA is lying until it proves it is telling the truth. Only time will tell who is lying—Edward Snowden or the National Security Agency. If anyone cares by then.

12

DEMONIZATION

Snowden: Spy, Traitor, Criminal

When Snowden took temporary asylum in Hong Kong, Dick Cheney attacked. "I'm suspicious because he went to China," Cheney told Fox News. "That's not a place where you would ordinarily go if you are interested in freedom, liberty, and so forth. It raises the question whether or not he had that kind of connection before he did this. . . . [The Chinese] would probably be willing to provide immunity for him or sanctuary for him in exchange for what he presumably knows or doesn't know."

◆

Edward Snowden is a spy.

Cheney's inaccurate accusation—Hong Kong is not China—was a typical damage-control ploy. Make an allegation disguised as a suspicion. Offer no evidence. Make the suspicion sound logical and reasonable. Hope that the word "spy" burrows deep into the psyche of patriotic Americans.

Snowden has to take some responsibility for the China-spy allegation after revealing how deeply he and other NSA intelligence officers had hacked into coded computer systems in Hong Kong and mainland China. We might legitimately ask: If Snowden was willing to *publicly* reveal the existence of NSA cyberspying against the Chinese, what did he share *privately* with them? Did he give the Chinese a list of NSA listening posts outside the United States that specialized in China-hacking? Did he tell the Chinese how the NSA cracked their sophisticated codes? Did he reveal the names of NSA spies working inside China?

Snowden quickly dismissed the spy allegation. In a live chat with *Guardian* readers, he said, "This is a predictable smear that I anticipated before going public, as the U.S. media have a knee-jerk, RED-CHINA reaction to anything involving Hong Kong or the People's Republic of China. [It] is intended to distract from the issue of U.S. government misconduct. . . . I have had no contact with the Chinese government. . . . I only work with journalists. . . . Ask yourself, if I were a Chinese spy, why wouldn't I have flown directly to Beijing? I would be living in a palace petting a phoenix by now."

There is no evidence to date that Snowden shared NSA classified documents with or sold them to the Chinese. Although his secret files would be worth millions to a foreign intelligence operation, there is no evidence to date that Snowden ever received money from the Chinese or any other foreign country.

As soon as Snowden left Hong Kong for Moscow, his accusers dropped the China-spy allegations and focused on Russian-spy charges. Representative Mike Rogers, a Republican from Michigan, became the point man for the intelligence community. A former FBI agent and chairman of both the House Intelligence Committee and the Permanent Select Committee on Intelligence, Rogers, in widely reported comments before a gathering of key members of the British House of Commons, accused Snowden of "living in the loving arms" of Russian spies. Rogers went on to claim on NBC's *Meet the Press* that there wasn't one counterintelligence officer who didn't believe that Snowden was "under the influence of Russian intelligence services."

Former KGB double agent and defector Major Boris Karpichkov publicly supported Rogers's spy allegation. Karpichkov claimed that the Russians set Snowden up, then played him like a mark. As a self-proclaimed, highly trained cyberspy and code breaker, Karpichkov reasoned that Snowden should have seen a con coming.

Karpichkov is a formerly high-ranking member of the Latvian branch of the Soviet KGB. After the collapse of the USSR he became a double agent, supplying information about Latvia to Russia's new security service while also working for the new Latvian security service. In the late 1990s he fled to England, where he led the shadowy life of a freelance spy.

According to Karpichkov, Russian intelligence services opened a dossier on Snowden as early as 2007, while he was working undercover for the CIA in Geneva. Karpichkov said that, as a talented code breaker and hacker, Snowden was of special interest to the Russians. They targeted him as a possible defector but didn't approach him until he fled to Hong Kong and became vulnerable. Then, Russian spies posing as diplomats in Hong Kong tricked him into seeking asylum in Russia. Once Snowden landed in Moscow, the Russians provoked the United States into cancelling his passport, in effect making him a prisoner.

"He fell for it," Karpichkov said. "Now the Russians are extracting all the intelligence he possesses."

It appears that Karpichkov was correct—up to a point. Russia did approach Snowden with an offer of asylum while he was still in Hong Kong. He would be safe in Russia because the country does not have an extradition treaty with the United States and, therefore, by law, it could not hand him over to the U.S. Department of Justice. For its part, China warned Snowden that the U.S. Department of State was about to revoke his passport, and that it was applying tremendous pressure on Hong Kong to arrest and detain him. Furthermore, Snowden's Hong Kong visa was good only for ninety days. It was clear to Edward Snowden, his attorneys, and his WikiLeaks advisers that he had to do something soon.

Snowden accepted the Russian asylum offer while he was in Hong Kong. His advisers were worried that the U.S. government would use Snowden's asylum in Russia as a pretext to label him a Russian spy. Snowden needed a ruse to make it look as though his choice of Russia was unplanned. The scenario they came up with was straight out of James Bond.

They told the media that Snowden would leave Hong Kong on June 23 on Russian Aeroflot Flight SU213 destined for Moscow. There he would be boarding another Aeroflot flight to Havana en route to Ecuador, which had offered him asylum. He carried a safe-passage letter issued by the Ecuadorian Embassy in London. The document was probably obtained by WikiLeaks, which paid for Snowden's flight from Hong Kong to Moscow. The transit document was worthless. It was neither approved nor signed by the government of Ecuador. But the media bought the story.

Eager reporters filled the plane Snowden was scheduled to take from Moscow to Havana. As predicted, the U.S. Department of State revoked Snowden's passport while he was en route to Moscow. Once he landed at Sheremetyevo International Airport, he couldn't leave the airport because he didn't have valid papers. He was marooned in the neutral transit area—a man without a country and a virtual prisoner

Edward Snowden then formally requested asylum in Russia. What choice did he have? To make the scenario realistic, Russian authorities let Snowden eat and sleep in the airport for five weeks, while they appeared to be debating the asylum issue. Then they offered a safe harbor for only one year, so that they would not appear too eager to have him. When the year was up, Russia extended asylum for three more years, until August 1, 2017. At the same time, Russian authorities gave Snowden permission to travel as long as he didn't remain outside the country for more than three months. His girlfriend, Lindsay Mills, visits him regularly.

Did the U.S. State Department cancel Snowden's passport so that he would be stuck in Russia, allowing the U.S. to claim that he was a Russian spy? Under pressure from Washington, did Cuba tell Moscow it would not allow the Russian plane carrying Snowden to touch down in Havana? Did Russian intelligence agencies orchestrate the scenario so that Snowden would be stuck in Russia, giving them an opportunity to exploit him? Did Snowden know the details of the ruse? Did he play a role in crafting it?

Snowden told the media that the State and Justice departments set him up. "My government revoked my passport intentionally to leave me exiled," he said in an interview at his Moscow apartment with two reporters from *The Nation* magazine. "If they really wanted to trap me, they would have allowed me to travel to Latin America, because the CIA can operate with impunity down there. They did not want that. They chose to keep me in Russia."

As a highly trained disinformation expert, Karpichkov was a perfect character assassin. The fact that he was an unreliable spy who could play both sides with skill and ease was beside the point. He *sounded* credible. And he made Congressman Rogers *look* credible. To date there is no evidence that Snowden supplied or sold information to Russian intelligence services. As the *New York Times* succinctly put it: "There has been no public indication that investigators of the FBI, NSA, or the Pentagon have uncovered evidence that Mr. Snowden received assistance from any foreign intelligence service."

Although Snowden admits that Russian intelligence officers approached him when he arrived in Moscow, he denies accepting their offer. He maintains that he did not bring a single classified file into Russia, that he has "no relationship with the Russian government [and] gets no financial support from the Russian government, and does not need it." Ben Wisner, an American Civil Liberties Union (ACLU) attorney representing Snowden at the time Congressman Rogers made the sweeping spy allegation, clarified his client's comment: "When Snowden says that he has 'no relationship' with the Russian government," Wisner said, "he means that he hasn't cooperated with their intelligence service in any way and that his asylum isn't conditioned on cooperation."

Snowden supports himself with savings, prize money, and speaking fees. He constructed a recording studio in his Moscow apartment so that he can teleconference interviews and speeches. He works as a computer maintenance technician at one of Russia's largest websites. Both Snowden and his Russian lawyer have declined to identify the web site for security reasons.

Snowden candidly admits that indeed he was a spy—for the United States. "I'm not some low-level hacker," he says to the demonizers who have tried to minimize his skill in an attempt to undermine his credibility. "It seems to me spies probably look a lot more like Ed Snowden and a lot less like James Bond these days. . . . I was trained as a spy in the traditional sense of the word, in that I lived and worked undercover, overseas, pretending to work in a job that I'm not and being assigned a name that was not mine."

✦

Edward Snowden is a traitor.

The list of Washington heavies who have accused Snowden of treason reads like a political *"Who's Who."* The lineup includes former vice president Dick Cheney; Democratic senator Dianne Feinstein from California, vice chairman of the Senate Select Committee on Intelligence; departing Republican House Speaker John Boehner; Republican representative Peter T. King from New York, former chairman of the House Committee on Homeland Security and a member of the House Permanent Committee on Intelligence; Republican senator Saxby Chambliss from Georgia, senior member of the Senate Select Committee on

Intelligence; Republican John Bolton, former U.S. ambassador to the United Nations; NSA point man Rick Ledgett; and the ubiquitous congressman Mike Rogers.

According to *Black's Law Dictionary*, a traitor is a person who is guilty of treason, "the offense of attempting to overthrow the government of the state to which one owes allegiance, either by making war against the state or by materially supporting its enemies." By that definition, Edward Snowden is not a traitor: he has not been tried and found guilty of treason.

The ACLU and other privacy activist supporters of Snowden see these attacks as a panicked attempt to wrest control of the storyline from Snowden in order to turn public opinion against him. The traitor accusation raises a question that Snowden critics and enemies choose to dodge. Can they actually prove it or are they merely engaging in reckless character assassination shielded by government immunity?

To explain why Snowden is a traitor, his critics parade before the public a list of specific and highly charged allegations. These can be grouped in three categories: revealing protected intelligence sources and methods; teaching terrorists how to adapt and reshape their tradecraft; and endangering the lives of U.S. and British intelligence officers. Each charge is a violation of Section 793 of the Espionage Act of 1917, which states that it is a treasonable crime to take, keep, and/or transfer knowledge "with intent, or reason to believe, that the information is to be used to injure the United States, or to the advantage of any foreign nation."

Congressman Rogers told a group of select members of the British House of Commons that our enemies changed their methods of communication, making it difficult to track them, because of the Snowden leaks. As a result, he said, it is now more likely that soldiers are "going to get their legs blown off or [be] killed. . . . That's murder. . . . Anybody that provides that information to the enemies is a traitor, period, pure and simple." Rogers further alleged that over 95 percent of the information Snowden leaked to the media has nothing to do with the NSA spying on the private communications of Americans or Europeans. They were "about tactical things, military plans and operations."

Rick Ledgett warned that the damage to U.S. national security caused by Snowden leaks "should not be underestimated." He accused Snowden of aiding "rival nations" by drawing a "roadmap of what we know, what we don't know," thus giving them a "way to protect their information from [the] U.S. intelligence community's view."

Senator Chambliss told *Meet the Press*: "[Snowden] needs to look an American jury in the eyes and explain why he has disclosed sources and methods that are going to put American lives in danger. . . . [W]e know now that because of his disclosure that the terrorists—the bad guys around the world—are taking some different tactics, and they know a little bit more about how we're gathering information on them."

John Bolton, former U.S. ambassador to the United Nations, compared Edward Snowden to Benedict Arnold. "We do not yet know whether Snowden jeopardized [security agents], but vital sources and methods of intelligence gathering and operations are clearly at risk," Bolton wrote. "In cyber terms, this is akin to Benedict Arnold scheming to betray West Point's defenses to the British, thereby allowing them to seize a key American fortification, splitting the colonies geographically at a critical point during the American

Revolution."

Note that the Department of Justice has not, as of this writing, charged Snowden with treason under the Espionage Act of 1917, as expanded by the Patriot Act of 2001. We can reasonably assume that if federal prosecutors had convincing evidence of treasonable acts, they would already have indicted him for treason.

Snowden's response to the traitor allegation borders on cavalier. "Being called a traitor by Dick Cheney is the highest honor you can give an American," he said, "and the more panicked talk we hear from people like him, Feinstein, and King, the better off we all are. . . . I am neither a traitor nor a hero. I'm an American."

While congressional and intelligence leaders mounted an aggressive attack on Snowden as a traitor, senior intelligence officials who spoke on condition of anonymity launched an aggressive counterdefense of NSA programs. In an exclusive interview with the Associated Press, they claimed that information the NSA gleaned through the PRISM and BOUNDLESS INFORMANT programs thwarted fifty potential terrorist plots, ten of which were "homeland-based threats."

NSA director Keith Alexander, whose motto was "Collect it All," was even more specific in his congressional testimonies. He told a House Intelligence Committee that agency surveillance programs helped uncover a plot to bomb the New York subway system. He pointed out that this was just one of the fifty terrorist attacks in twenty countries that NSA's bulk collection of phone and e-mail communications had thwarted. NSA congressional supporters Dianne Feinstein and Mike Rogers made a similar claim about the capture of David Headley, who was sentenced in January 2015 to thirty-five years in jail for his role in the 2008 terrorist attacks in Mumbai, India, that killed 168 people.

Both claims were distorted.

According to the government version, the FBI foiled a 2009 al-Qaeda plot to blow up the New York subway during the morning rush hour. The Bureau claimed that its snoop program intercepted an e-mail from a known Pakistani member of al-Qaeda to Najibullah Zazi, an Afghan-American terrorist living in Colorado. The e-mail described recipes for explosives. FBI agents followed Zazi to New York. Search warrants turned up bomb components. Zazi subsequently confessed to plotting to blow up the city's subway system with a backpack bomb.

In reality, Americans have the British to thank for saving the New York subway and countless lives, not NSA's warrantless data sweeps. British intelligence agents learned about Zazi during an Operation Pathway investigation into a suspected terrorist cell in northwest England. (Pathway was a legally sanctioned program to electronically snoop on known or suspected terrorists without having to obtain a specific warrant to do so.) Pathway investigators discovered that a member of the cell had been in contact with an al-Qaeda associate in Pakistan. British intelligence agents passed the tip and the Pakistani's e-mail address to American intelligence agents, who began tracking the al-Qaeda terrorist. His e-mails led them to Zazi.

Americans also have the British to thank for the capture of David Headley, a Pakistani-American from Chicago, who was plotting to attack the Danish paper *Jyllands-Posten* in retaliation for its 2006 publication of cartoons of the Prophet

Mohammed, which Muslims found offensive. Once British agents picked up Headley's trail, they tipped off American intelligence officers. NSA data-mining sweeps had nothing to do with finding Headley. "That's nonsense," an anonymous American agent, who worked the case, told the *Guardian*. "It played no role at all."

Simply put, the NSA, FBI, and CIA didn't need bulk data mining to investigate Zazi's and Headley's phone records and e-mails. Their agents already had authority under the Patriot Act to intercept the phone and e-mail messages of Zazi and Headley without obtaining a warrant to do so, once they identified them as terrorist suspects.

FBI director Robert Mueller used the same playbook as Keith Alexander. He told a House judicial oversight committee that the bulk collection of data on phone calls is an essential part of U.S. counterterrorism. He went on to claim that electronic surveillance of Americans could have prevented 9/11 and would prevent another Boston Marathon bombing. "If we lose our ability to get [terrorist] communications," Mueller testified, "we are going to be exceptionally vulnerable."

Senator Mark Udall of Colorado, a member of the Senate Intelligence Committee, summarized the security-versus-privacy debate in a statement he issued after one of Alexander's congressional appearances: "We have not yet seen any evidence showing that NSA's dragnet collection of Americans' phone records has produced any uniquely valuable intelligence. . . . All the plots that he mentioned appear to have been identified using other collection methods. The public deserves a clear explanation."

Like NSA's Keith Alexander, Sir Iain Lobban, head of

Britain's intelligence agency, GCHQ, mounted a fierce attack on Edward Snowden. Lobban told the British Intelligence and Security Committee that terrorists "are rubbing their hands with glee" after the Snowden leaks and adopting more secure forms of communication to hatch their plots. He went on to claim that, based on the intelligence data collected in bulk, GCHQ had thwarted a total of thirty-four terror plots—some major—between the July 7, 2005, bloody subway attack in London's Underground and November 2013. According to sources in the office of the prime minister and in intelligence agencies, Britain has now pulled agents out of live operations in "hostile countries" after Russia and China hacked into Snowden's files. Those sources believe that the documents China and Russia cracked would compromise the lives of British and American spies.

Like NSA's General Alexander and FBI's Robert Mueller, Sir Iain Lobban offered the British no evidence to support his claims that bulk data mining was thwarting terrorist plots. And he presented no proof that Russian and Chinese hackers had broken into Snowden's cache of classified NSA documents and files.

✦

Ironically, it was Snowden himself who gave his enemies and critics grounds for calling him a traitor. In an exclusive interview with the *South China Morning Post* (SCMP) soon after he outed himself, Snowden shared with the daily newspaper "unverified" documents showing that the "NSA has been hacking computers in Hong Kong and on the mainland since 2009."

The documents dealt with U.S. spying on civilian targets—universities, public officials, businesses, and students. One of NSA's major civilian targets in mainland China was Unicom, the nation's second-largest communication provider, with 258 million users. Another civilian target was Tsinghua University in Beijing. The school was important because, as author Michael Gurnow points out, "it houses the world's largest national research portal, the Chinese Education and Research Network." Snowden told SCMP that he chose to leak the classified documents to demonstrate "the hypocrisy of the U.S. government when it claims that it does not target civilian infrastructure, unlike its adversaries." His explanation was consistent with his stated goal: to share his classified NSA documents with the media, not with government, and to release only those documents that showed how the NSA was spying on suspicionless targets.

Then Snowden went on to tell SCMP that there were more than 61,000 NSA hacking operations globally, with hundreds of targets in Hong Kong and on the Chinese mainland. "We hack network backbones—like huge internet routers," he said, "that give us access to the communications of hundreds of thousands of computers without having to hack every one." Critics like John Bolton were quick to respond. "What Americans should understand most importantly is what the China leaks reveal about Snowden," Bolton wrote in a special to the *Guardian* a few days after Snowden's interview with the Chinese daily. "If he is lying about these programs . . . that tells us something important about his character. And if he is telling the truth, revealing sensitive information about American efforts to protect itself against the world's greatest cyber-warfare power, that tells us even more about his character. . . . Is he now, both overtly and covertly, trying to bribe Beijing's authorities to secure asylum in China, contrary to his earlier smug comments about facing the consequences of his actions in America? . . . Make no mistake: any American politician who now calls Snowden a hero is not fit to be entrusted with America's national security."

In March, 2014, Snowden leaked to the *Washington Post* documents describing another top-secret bulk collection program called MYSTIC. Through MYSTIC, the NSA was collecting "every single" phone conversation in a politically sensitive foreign country. The *Post* withheld the name of that country at the request of U.S. officials, who argued that disclosure would irreparably harm national security.

Two months later, WikiLeaks—not known for discretion—revealed the name of that country—Afghanistan. The disclosure forced intelligence officials to terminate MYSTIC in that country. According to James Clapper, director of National Intelligence, MYSTIC "was the single most important source of force protection and warning for our people in Afghanistan."

When Snowden has chosen to leak top-secret, classified reports, he leaves it up to the media to act responsibly. According to Clapper, the Post did. WikiLeaks did not. The name of Afghanistan raises three thorny questions. Did Snowden leak MYSTIC documents to WikiLeaks? If he did, was he acting responsibly? How many U.S. soldiers and Afghanis have been or may be killed as a result?

◆

What Alexander, Mueller, Ledgett, Bolton, King, Rogers, and others didn't say is that NSA insiders doubted the value of PRISM and BOUNDLESS INFORMANT. Months before the Snowden leaks, the agency had already scrapped BOUNDLESS INFORMANT because its cost outweighed its benefits. And while Snowden was leaking NSA documents, agency intelligence managers were debating whether to recommend scuttling PRISM as well because, they concluded, its cost outweighed the "meager counterintelligence benefits."

✦

Edward Snowden is a criminal.

Damage controllers point out that Snowden acknowledged stealing highly classified documents and giving them to the media in violation of the criminal code. That makes him an admitted criminal. In answer to the accusation of criminality, Snowden argues that breaking a law that is itself criminal doesn't make him a criminal. He believes he did the right thing even if the law says he didn't.

A comparable situation is that of a terminally ill wife, in pain, who begs her husband to help her die. He does. He breaks the law. A jury will find him guilty, even though some members might do the same thing under similar circumstances. The jury merely does what the law requires. The husband will accept the expected verdict. The judge will sentence him as required. The law is the law. But in his heart, the husband knows he is no criminal.

Snowden fully understands his predicament. "I could not do this without accepting the risk of prison," he told the *Guardian.* "You can't come up against the world's most powerful intelligence agencies and not accept the risk. If they want to get you, over time they will." Snowden then went on to defend his actions. "We have seen enough criminality on the part of the government," he says. "It is hypocritical to make this allegation against me."

The government has charged Snowden with three counts of criminal activity, but he has not been convicted of any charge, nor has he formally pled guilty. Therefore, we can legitimately say only that he is an *alleged* criminal under indictment. Lawyers who have studied the Espionage Act of 1917 are quick to point out that there is no practical defense against the sweeping law that prohibits the revealing of national security information "to any person not entitled to receive it." The law makes no exceptions.

"As much as some may want Snowden to be applauded for his actions, as a legal matter, his self-stated laudable intentions are irrelevant to his criminal liability," Washington attorney Mark Zaid argued. "He can only hope that it will play a role in his sentencing. Having publicly self-admitted his guilt for having illegally leaked classified information, he has eliminated any likely meaningful defense."

If Snowden is tried under the Espionage Act of 1917, he will most likely be convicted and sentenced as was Ethel Rosenberg, who was executed in the electric chair for giving secret information about the atomic bomb to the Soviet Union, and Chelsea (Bradley) Manning, who was sentenced to thirty-five years in prison (with the possibility of parole in eight) for giving classified documents to WikiLeaks. Snowden's best option would be to convince at least one juror that his leaks were justified because he acted in good faith and followed his conscience. If jury nullification—a realistic possibility given the recent surge of sympathy for

Snowden—is Snowden's only possibility to avoid jail, the heart of his trial would be jury selection, with each side rejecting and selecting those jurors who would best support their arguments.

In the end, the Snowden affair embodies a hypothetical irony and asks a dicey question. Ironically, if Snowden is eventually tried in the United States and sent to prison, and if the courts find the NSA guilty of criminal and/or unconstitutional intelligence gathering, Snowden would remain behind bars because he broke a law when he exposed the criminal and or unconstitutional behavior. Yet those government officials deemed guilty of the criminal and/or constitutional invasion of privacy might never be punished.

The question is: Is there a higher law?

13

A HIGHER LAW?

Snowden focused his torch beam on a decision-making topic that lawmakers, politicians, and the intelligence community avoid—the existence of a higher law. Their law of choice, more often than not, is political expediency. Snowden challenged them to a public debate. "I cannot in good conscience," he said, "allow the U.S. government to destroy privacy, internet freedom, and basic liberties for people around the world with this massive surveillance machine they're secretly building."

Although there are many ways of defining "higher law"—some of which have deep religious connotations—everyone can accept one definition. Higher law is conscience, or that human faculty that recognizes the difference between right and wrong and is accompanied by an inner voice that urges us to choose right instead of wrong. We can listen to our conscience and follow it. Or we can deny it and suffer nagging, sometimes guilt-ridden consequences.

One path to following our conscience is civil disobedience. *Black's Law Dictionary* defines that as "the refusal to obey a law because it is thought to be unfair or undesirable." Did Edward Snowden commit an act of civil disobedience when he leaked classified documents to the media? Civil disobedience has a set of well-defined criteria.

To qualify as civil disobedience, an act must be illegal. Snowden stole classified documents and gave them to the media, a violation of the U.S. Criminal Code.

An act of civil disobedience must have been taken for a moral or ethical reason. Snowden said that he blew the whistle on the NSA because morally it was the right thing to do.

The intent of civil disobedience must be to change the law. Snowden said that he wanted the privacy laws already in place to be obeyed, the legality and constitutionality of NSA's secret snooping to be debated and tested, and Americans to be given the right to demand stricter privacy protection laws.

The person who breaks the law through civil disobedience must be willing to accept punishment. Snowden has said that he is willing to go to prison if he can get a fair trial.

The act of civil disobedience must be nonviolent. Snowden has not physically hurt anyone directly.

Finally, civil disobedience must be the last resort. Snowden has claimed that he tried to correct alleged NSA abuses by voicing his concerns to a string of NSA superiors and colleagues over a period of months. When they didn't act, he turned to the media and thus broke the law.

Based on those criteria, Snowden committed an act of civil disobedience. This conclusion raises another thorny question. Is civil disobedience a heroic option or a moral duty? We need go no further than Henry David Thoreau for a thoughtful, challenging discussion of the issue. One hundred and fifty years ago, he published a pamphlet titled *On the Duty of Civil Disobedience,* protesting war and slavery, which his conscience told him were illegal government behaviors. He refused to pay the taxes that supported those behaviors and was sent to jail.

Not everyone will agree with Thoreau's probing questions about the role of government, the necessity of civil disobedience, or his moral conclusion. But his argument deserves to be heard in the context of the highly debated civil disobedience of Edward Snowden. Thoreau had a deeply held bias, which he throws down like a gauntlet, unlike those who camouflage the biases underlying their works. Like libertarians today, Thoreau believed that government is at its best when it governs least. He wrote:

> The government itself, which is only the mode which people have chosen to execute their will, is equally liable to be abused and perverted before the people can act through it. . . .
>
> Must the citizen ever for a moment, or in the least degree, resign his conscience to the legislator? Why has every man a conscience then? I think we should be men first and subjects afterwards. . . .
>
> Law never made men a whit more just; and, by means of respect for it, even the well-disposed are daily made agents of injustice. . . .
>
> Most legislators, politicians, lawyers, ministers, and office holders serve the State chiefly with their heads; and, as they rarely make any moral distinc-

tion, they are as likely to serve the devil (without intending it) as God. . . .

Unjust laws exist. Shall we be content to obey them, or shall we endeavor to amend and obey them until we have succeeded, or shall we transgress them at once. . . .

It cost me less . . . to incur the penalty of disobedience to the State than it would to obey. I should feel as if I was worth less in that case. . . .

[The State] is not armed with superior wit or honesty, but with superior strength. I was not born to be forced. . . .

There will never be a really free and enlightened State until the State comes to recognize the individual as a higher and independent power, from which all its own power and authority are derived. . . .

The only obligation which I have a right to assume is to do at any time what I think is right.

Snowden critics point out that Thoreau's argument for civil disobedience, based on the dictates of conscience, has a fatal flaw: it assumes that the inner voice of conscience is reasonable, true, honest, and just. What if that voice is misguided? What if it is evil? Take the mother who kills her daughter because her conscience tells her the child is possessed by the devil and must be set free. Or the abortion opponent whose conscience says that abortion is murder and therefore abortion doctors are murderers who deserve to be killed. Or the serial killer of gay men who hears God telling him to kill them because they are an abomination. Granted, these are extreme examples ripped from headlines, but they illustrate the point. Just because we hear an inner voice telling us what's right or wrong doesn't mean that the inner voice is correct or moral.

Critics argue that Edward Snowden's conscience told him to reveal government secrets that impinge on the lives of all Americans and are vital to protect Americans from terrorist attacks. Who gives him the right to speak for the nation? Isn't it the pinnacle of hubris to say that I, Edward Snowden, know best?

14

DEMONIZATION

Silkwood: Heartless Mother, Drug Addict, Mentally Unstable, Plutonium Smuggler, Liar

If Edward Snowden fails to give his enemies any useful dirt about his personal life, Silkwood makes up for it. Her demonizers didn't have to dig. They accused her of being a heartless mother who abandoned her children: how could you trust a woman who didn't fight for custody of her kids? Of being a druggie who smoked grass and overdosed on prescribed medication—that made her a criminal. Of deliberately contaminating herself with plutonium to embarrass Kerr-McGee. Wasn't that mental instability? They claimed Silkwood was part of a plutonium smuggling ring at the Cimarron plant. That made her a terrorist. They said she had no solid proof that Kerr-McGee was fudging on quality control. That made her a liar. They said she attempted suicide more than once. You couldn't trust anyone so unstable. And they said that while high on prescribed medication, Karen Silkwood fell asleep at the wheel of her Honda and lost control of the car. She was responsible for her own death.

After Silkwood's death, Kerr-McGee security director

James Reading circulated a three-page document with at-
tachments outlining the "charges" against her. Undated and
unsigned, it was widely quoted in the media and during 1976
hearings before the House Subcommittee on Energy and the
Environment that dealt with mishandling of plutonium at
U.S. nuclear facilities like the Kerr-McGee Cimarron plant.

Were the allegations against Karen Silkwood true or distorted? Fair or foul?

✦

Karen Silkwood abandoned her children.

Legally, child abandonment is an act in which a parent
deserts a child without any regard for the child's physical
health, safety, or welfare. Karen Silkwood did not do that.
On an August morning in 1972 she walked out on her troubled marriage and never came back. She legally relinquished
custody of her three children to her husband, a condition he
demanded for an uncontested divorce. He had the means to
guarantee the health, safety, and welfare of their children.
The divorce court awarded Silkwood visitation rights.

✦

Karen Silkwood was a drug addict.

Karen Silkwood was one of eight million Americans
who regularly smoked marijuana in the mid-1970s. Her
drug use was not a secret. After her death, Kerr-McGee
investigators questioned her coworkers, acquaintances,
and enemies, several of whom said that they had seen her
"high" in social settings. But however much grass she may

have smoked privately, no one ever filed a complaint against Silkwood for being high on the job. During the more than two years she worked at the Cimarron plant, she was reprimanded only once, and that was for taking a prescribed medication at work without informing her supervisor, as required.

While packing up Silkwood's contaminated belongings for burial in a radioactive dump, Kerr-McGee investigators who were looking for evidence to use against her found a syringe, considered proof that she was injecting herself with narcotics. They sent the syringe to a lab for analysis. It tested negative. Silkwood had used it as a turkey baster.

While rifling through Silkwood's personal papers, investigators struck pay dirt with an undated, itemized household budget in her handwriting that listed $300 for "dope." In the early 1970s that was enough to buy about a pound of cheap, commercial-grade grass. Given the other items in the budget (rent, telephone, etc.), it could be considered an allowance for a particular month. There is no indication, however, that she set aside $300 for dope every month. Nor is there any evidence that "dope" meant heroin or cocaine, or that she sold marijuana to her friends or fellow workers. Silkwood critics have also pointed out that she had two joints in her purse the night she was killed.

There is no doubt that Silkwood was abusing legal prescription drugs. Pharmacy and doctor records show that she was consuming more Quaaludes, prescribed as sleeping pills, than recommended. She took them as stress relievers during the day. Medical examiners found half of a partially digested Quaalude in her stomach the night she was killed. She also overdosed on pills and passed out at least twice. Kerr-McGee interpreted the overdosing as deliberate attempts to take her life. She wrote no suicide notes.

✦

Karen Silkwood was mentally unstable.

Kerr–McGee accused Karen Silkwood of deliberately contaminating herself with plutonium to embarrass the company. If she did so, she would also have committed the crime of stealing the plutonium that contaminated her in her apartment a week before she was killed. If charged and found guilty, she would have been sentenced to prison. Kerr–McGee and the FBI argued that there were three possible motives for the self-contamination they alleged. Either Silkwood was furious with Kerr–McGee about the reprimand she got for taking a prescribed medication on the job without reporting it, or she was spying on Kerr–McGee for the union, hoping to find documents that would embarrass the company, and when she couldn't find any, chose to manufacture a misdeed. Or the union had become an obsession for Silkwood, who, under pressure and in distress, contaminated herself to help the union.

The Criminal Division of the Justice Department commissioned the FBI to investigate Silkwood's contamination as a crime of plutonium theft. According to an investigative file obtained under a Freedom of Information Act request, FBI investigators worked under a single premise—that Karen Silkwood contaminated herself. They scoured for evidence to prove it. They studied lab records that indicated a series of her urine samples had been spiked with insoluble plutonium. After they traced the pellet lot that the plutonium came from, it was clear that almost anyone at the plant could have taken enough to salt Silkwood's kits, which were labeled with her name and badge number and sat on an open shelf. They interviewed workers to see if anyone saw her take plutonium. And they reported that even her boyfriend, Drew, had doubts. He told the FBI that on their trip to Los Alamos for Karen's full-body radiation count he felt compelled to ask her if she had swallowed a plutonium pellet. She assured him that she hadn't.

After the FBI investigation was completed, the Bureau compiled a fifty-page report that proved Silkwood was contaminated in her apartment with plutonium stolen from the Cimarron plant. But as hard as it had tried, the FBI could not prove that she was the one who had stolen it.

Silkwood supporters label the self-contamination charge character assassination. Their case is purely emotional and psychological: Silkwood understood that plutonium causes cancer, so why would she swallow it? She couldn't stop crying when she found out how severely she had been contaminated. When she called Steve Wodka to tell him what had happened in her apartment, she was crying so hard that he could barely understand her. Between sobs in a phone call to her mother she said that she was dying and that she would be coming home. She refused to kiss Drew because she was afraid she might contaminate him. And she placed her soiled sanitary napkins in a plastic bag to protect others and the environment.

Does this sound like a woman who deliberately swallowed a plutonium pellet?

Kerr–McGee had five years—1974 to 1979—to prepare a case that would sow the seeds of probable doubt in the minds of the jury during the eight-week negligence trial, or prove that Karen Silkwood had deliberately contaminated herself. When the jury filed into the courtroom after reaching a verdict, the clerk read the questions Judge Frank Theis had asked the panel to ponder. The first question was, "Do you find by a preponderance of the evidence that Karen Silkwood intentionally—that is, knowingly and consciously—carried from work to her apartment the plutonium that caused her contamination?"

"No!" the jury foreman said.

◆

Plutonium smuggler.

The FBI and OSBI began spying on Silkwood as a plutonium smuggler either in late 1972 during the OCAW strike or in early 1973 after the strike was settled, nearly two years before she died. The Bureau would later add Drew and Karen's roommate, Sherri Ellis, to its list of suspected smugglers. The final word on the Bureau investigation is not yet in. In response to a 2012 FOIA request, the U.S. National Archives declassified an FBI investigative file on plutonium smuggling at the Cimarron plant. To date, three hundred pages of the file, covering 1974 to mid-1975, have been declassified. Thirty-seven additional pages from that time period remain classified after forty years. Another four hundred pages, covering mid-1975 through 1982, are still classified as well.

The FBI originally opened the plutonium smuggling investigation around the end of 1972 or the beginning of 1973 because approximately forty pounds of plutonium were missing from the plant. Bureau investigators concluded that the material unaccounted for (MUF) was not removed from the Cimarron plant all at once. Inventory reports showed an ever-growing MUF figure, which suggested an ongoing operation of some sophistication. Since the plutonium was not properly secured, almost anyone in the plant—worker, manager, AEC official, or government intelligence officer assigned to hunt terrorists—could have wrapped the highly radioactive substance in tinfoil and walked out of the plant without being detected. That the FBI had homed in on plutonium *smuggling* is a clear indication that it had ruled out two other possibilities—that the MUF was an accounting error or that it went out as plant waste to be buried in a radioactive dump, as Kerr-McGee and the AEC claimed.

Bill Taylor, the Silkwood family's investigator, had a source, "Echo," with top security clearance, inside FBI headquarters in Washington. To date, no one has come forward to seriously challenge the information Echo passed on to Taylor. Echo cautioned Taylor not to rule out CIA involvement in the Silkwood case because the CIA was directly involved in monitoring the nuclear industry. (The listening device that Tony Mazzocchi found behind his kitchen clock was a CIA variety.) Echo went on to tell Taylor that the security director of each U.S. nuclear facility was under CIA surveillance, and that Kerr-McGee would have had to deal directly or indirectly with the agency before it was awarded any contract to work with plutonium.

Echo's CIA observations were logical and made sense from an intelligence standpoint. But Echo told Taylor next that the CIA had been diverting plutonium from nuclear plants and giving it to countries friendly to the United

States. Echo further said that a number of CIA agents had been contaminated with the plutonium they had diverted. Several had even died. And Echo added that he didn't know if the CIA had taken plutonium from the Kerr-McGee Cimarron plant because he did not have direct access to that particular report.

Echo's diverted-plutonium observations have not been taken seriously because he offered no evidence or documents to prove CIA diversion. It is outside the scope of this book to seek answers to how many pounds of highly enriched uranium and plutonium still remain unaccounted for, and how much (if any) has been diverted to U.S. allies, especially Israel—a politically sensitive issue.

What is known, however, is that U.S. nuclear scientists have been trying to get answers to those two questions since the 1950s. Few classified files dealing with MUF investigations have been fully declassified to date, and the public record is filled with holes and contradictions. Although the Kerr-McGee Cimarron plant closed more than forty years ago, no terrorist has yet used a dirty bomb fueled by plutonium. Nor has anyone offered proof that Echo was wrong.

Curiously, one of Bill Taylor's other intelligence sources offered him a tip that he followed up: to check out the hanger at a small, nontowered airport outside San Diego. There Taylor found a sensitive laboratory metric scale on a shelf. On the bottom of it was a sticker that said "Kerr-McGee." He then noted several phone numbers scrawled on the wall next to a pay phone. One had a 202 area code—Washington, D.C. It was the number for the Israeli Embassy.

◆

Karen Silkwood was a liar.

A month after Silkwood's death, the AEC released the results of its investigation into quality control at the Cimarron plant. AEC inspector Kenneth H. Jackson had examined three Silkwood allegations: falsification of negatives and photos of fuel-rod welds; falsification of quality-control analytical data; and faulty pellet inspection. Given the fact that he worked out of the AEC's corrupt Chicago regional office, Jackson's findings might be considered highly suspect.

An unnamed lab analyst at the Cimarron plant admitted to Jackson that he had been touching up quality-control negatives with a felt-tipped pen from February to June 1974. (In September 1974 Silkwood told OCAW about the doctored negatives.) The analyst told Jackson that none of the touch-ups disguised serious flaws in the weld seals, that he was working alone, and that Kerr-McGee management didn't know about the doctoring.

Although Jackson found fifty-three photographs printed from doctored negatives, his report did not indicate that he had checked to see if the touch-ups were minor (as the analyst claimed), or whether they covered up serious flaws. He did not report whether he interviewed Cimarron plant managers or Westinghouse managers at Hanford, Washington, to see if they had spotted irregular fuel-rod welds. He stated that he found no evidence of fraudulent written quality-control records, but he failed to say what kind of records he reviewed, how many, and what period of time those records covered.

Finally, Jackson reported that none of the workers who shaped and weighed pellets admitted cutting corners. They told him that they had diligently followed AEC guidelines even when Kerr-McGee sped up production. One of the workers, according to Jackson, was Silkwood's friend Jean Young, who knew about defective pellets and defective pellet lot 223. Young swore in a deposition taken several years after Silkwood's death that she was never interviewed by Jackson or any other AEC inspector.

When Karen Silkwood blew the whistle to the AEC managers in Bethesda, Maryland, she alleged thirty-nine specific health and safety violations at the Cimarron plant and provided details—names, dates, times, and descriptions. As promised after the Bethesda meeting, the AEC investigated the allegations. It was able to verify twenty-nine. Silkwood had proven her credibility, her supporters argue.

Kerr-McGee further alleged that Silkwood didn't have documents with her on the night she died. But eyewitness evidence that she had a stack of documents that she intended to deliver to the *New York Times* is clear, consistent, and compelling. In her phone call with Steve Wodka the night before she was to meet with David Burnham of the *Times*, who was due to travel from Washington to Oklahoma City, she told him that she was ready for her meeting with Burnham.

"If you can't put it together," Wodka said, "I won't bring him down."

"Let's do it," she said.

The next morning, Wednesday, November 13, 1974, after attending the second bargaining session with Kerr-McGee, she went to an OCAW meeting in the back room of the Hub Café in Crescent. Jean Young sat close to her. "During the meeting, [Karen] was leafing through papers in a folder," Young later testified in a sworn deposition. "I watched her doing this, and noticed that some of the papers were quite heavy—almost like cardboard—and smaller than typewriter paper. These looked to me like they might be photographs. . . . She had told me one day she had photographs of defective welds on sample fuel-pin claddings taken from lots which were passed by quality control. She once told me about a particularly bad batch of rods. I believe it was lot 223—which she said should never have been allowed to leave the plant."

After the meeting ended at around seven, Silkwood told Young that she was dying of cancer. She pointed to a stack of documents sitting on the table—a dark brown legal-size folder made of heavy material like cardboard and a reddish-brown, 8½-by-11–inch spiral notebook. Silkwood said that these materials were proof about the falsification of quality-control records. A few minutes later, Silkwood climbed into her car and began the thirty-minute journey to Oklahoma City.

✦

A half hour later, a truck driver spotted a smashed Honda in a ditch. He pulled over, got out, and looked down at the body inside but could detect no movement. He noticed some papers on the ground and a purse resting against the retaining wall two feet in front of the car. Approximately thirty minutes after the truck driver reported the accident, Oklahoma Highway Patrol officer Rick Fagen arrived at the scene and climbed down into the ditch to see who was in the car and if she was alive. A rookie who had been on the job only five months, Fagen had investigated fewer than fifty accidents. He picked up the papers lying outside the car and tossed them into the front seat. Later that night, he met with Roy King, a Kerr-McGee manager.

Someone tried to murder Roy King before he could testify in a sworn deposition about what Fagen told him about Silkwood's documents that night and the following morning. His wife woke him in the middle of the night saying she was cold. When King got out of bed to check the furnace, he smelled gas. The gas was turned on but the flame was out. He turned the gas off before getting back in bed. The next morning, he called the gas company. A technician examined both the furnace and the meter and told King it was no accident. Someone had deliberately extinguished the flame. It's understandable that King, afraid someone would try to kill him again, begged Silkwood family attorneys not to depose him. They called him anyway, and he testified that Highway Patrolman Fagen had told him: "There's a lot of things in her car that have Kerr-McGee identification insignia on them. I would like you to join with me tomorrow and we will go down there [to the impounded Honda] and get those. . . . That next morning . . . here comes the highway patrolman. And he said, 'Well, someone had *got* those. So there's no need—any point in us going down there to pick them up.'"

Fagen would later say, "I don't recall saying any of that."

The Silkwood legal team was able to determine from eyewitnesses that both Kerr-McGee personnel and AEC inspectors (or intelligence officers posing as AEC inspectors) had examined Silkwood's impounded Honda a few hours after her death. The documents in her car disappeared.

Kerr-McGee attorneys planned to call witnesses to testify about the character flaws, crimes, and emotional state of Karen Silkwood as a crucial part of its defense in the negligence suit Silkwood's family brought against the company. The allegations never made it to the courtroom. During an in camera hearing after the plaintiff rested its case, Judge Frank Theis quashed the defense's planned attack. "It's character assassination," Theis ruled.

In sum, the allegations about Karen Silkwood's character were attempts on the part of Kerr-McGee, the AEC, and other powerful interests to blacken her name and make her the wrongdoer because they needed to divert attention from their own malfeasance.

15

ASLEEP AT THE WHEEL?

Silkwood

Silkwood demonizers allege that she was under the influence of drugs the night her car crashed into the cement wing wall and that it was, therefore, a one-car accident she herself caused when she fell asleep behind the wheel of her Honda and lost control. How did they arrive at that conclusion?

There were three Silkwood accident reports—the one prepared by Highway Patrolman Rick Fagen; the medical examiner's autopsy report; and an independent accident reconstruction report commissioned by OCAW.

✦

After the ambulance took Karen Silkwood's body to a local hospital and a wrecker pulled the car out of the ditch, Rick Fagen began hunting for clues. Flashlight in hand, he followed the Honda tracks from the wing wall to the point where it had left the road and entered the shoulder. He didn't find anything to note. Next, he walked one hundred feet up the highway looking for skid marks, glass, or debris that would indicate a hit-and-run. He didn't find any. To him, it looked as if the driver had fallen asleep at the wheel. But since it was too dark to see clearly and he had to find and notify next of kin, Fagen decided to come back the next day for a closer look.

At nine the next morning Fagen once again traced the Honda tracks in the grass on the shoulder. It looked as if the vehicle had entered it at a forty-five-degree angle, then straightened out and headed for the wing wall. Fagen concluded that Silkwood must have crossed Highway 74 from the right lane to the left shoulder at a forty-five-degree angle. He drew a diagram of the car's trajectory on his green accident form. He did not take pictures.

He again checked for skid marks. There were plenty at the corner where Highway 33 crossed 74. And there were rubber scuffs near an unpaved oil road. Since none of the scuffs matched his forty-five-degree-angle theory, he didn't bother to measure and photograph them. Finally, Fagen drove his patrol car slowly up the highway for five hundred feet, past the point where the Honda hit the left shoulder. He found nothing to help determine at what point the Honda began to leave the road.

Fagen left the accident site and drove into Crescent to examine the car, which was impounded at a Ford dealership lot. It was Fagen's job to collect personal items from the vehicle and to box and seal them for next of kin. If he examined the outside of the Honda for clues of a hit-and-run, it was a cursory look. He took no measurements. He didn't jack up the car to look underneath. He took no pictures.

Fagen found in the car a cigarette roller and a letter from

a friend in Ontario. The letter made references to marijuana and explained how to use the roller. He also found a plastic bottle containing a red liquid. Suspecting that it might be an alchoholic Bloody Mary mix, he sent a sample to a police lab for testing. The results, received after Fagen had filed his report, said the liquid was spoiled tomato juice.

From the Ford dealership, Fagen drove to the Cimarron plant, where Roy King, the plant personnel director, was waiting with two OCAW members who had attended the union meeting at the Hub Café. They told Fagen that Silkwood looked so tired and stressed that they offered her a ride home, which she declined. Fagen would later tell the FBI that witnesses told him Silkwood had been in an "extreme emotional condition." However, he never interviewed Jean Young or Alma Hall, who also had attended the meeting at the Hub and had chatted with Silkwood afterward. Both would later testify that Silkwood looked tired but that they had no reason to believe she couldn't drive safely.

The next day—two days after the death of Karen Silkwood—Rick Fagen filed an accident report. He put an X in the box labeled "drinking—ability impaired." Next to the box labeled "sleepy," he typed "drugs." In the section labeled "unsafe, unlawful," he typed "under the influence of drugs." On the bottom of the report, he wrote: "Witnesses interviewed stated that they had advised the driver was in no physical condition to operate a vehicle."

What evidence did Fagen have to support his conclusions? There were no skid marks in line with his forty-five-degree trajectory theory. Fagen concluded that Silkwood had fallen asleep and drifted left. Someone had told him she had driven all the way from Los Alamos the previous day and had arrived home late at night. Therefore, he concluded, she must have been sleepy. (Silkwood had flown back from Los Alamos.) A witness he did not identify in the report had told him Karen had been drinking at the Hub Café. (She had sipped iced tea, and the autopsy showed that she had only "insignificant traces of alcohol" in her blood left over from drinks consumed the night before.) Another witness, also not identified, said she was taking sleeping pills. There were two marijuana joints and one and a half capsules in her purse. Fagen concluded that her driving ability had been impaired by alcohol and that she was under the influence of drugs.

Who told Fagen that Silkwood had driven from Los Alamos? That she had been drinking alcohol at the Hub? That she was taking sleeping pills? During a sworn deposition taken several years later, Fagen, now a lieutenant, said that he couldn't recall. What he did recall was that Silkwood's car reeked of alcohol. If so, why didn't he include that in his accident report? And where did the odor come from if he found no alcohol in the car? No one who examined the Honda the night of the accident reported a smell of alcohol.

In Washington, OCAW legislative director Tony Mazzocchi and his associate Steve Wodka did not buy Fagen's report and its conclusions. With a nod from the president of the union, they hired A. O. Pipkin, the owner of Accident Reconstruction Laboratories in Dallas, to investigate the accident. Unlike Fagen, Pipkin was no rookie. He had picked his way around the scenes of more than two thousand crashes and had testified in three hundred court cases. And unlike Fagen, he made it a point not to interview eyewitnesses or the friends and associates of the deceased. He let the vehicles and the accident site do the talking.

◆

Adolphus O. Pipkin landed at the Oklahoma City airport on November 16, three days after Silkwood was killed. He carried a thick gray case filled with the standard tools of his trade—camera with assorted lenses, transit compass for angles and road grades, tape measure, folding tripod, camera clamp that bites on to trees or fenders or bridges. It was unusual for Pipkin to hunt for clues and evidence three days after an accident. He generally entered a case weeks or even months after crashes.

He began his investigation at the wing wall on Highway 74. He measured, studied, and photographed the Honda tracks on the left washboard shoulder and grass. He noted first that the Honda went off the *left side* of the road. In most one-car accidents, where the driver has fallen asleep or is under the influence of drugs or alcohol, the vehicle drifts to the *right* because of the contour, or crown, of the road. Second, Pipkin noted that the Honda tracks in the grass showed that the car had not *drifted* across the road. The turf was chewed up at the entry point and the car was yawing, or moving unsteadily, as it sped down the shoulder. The driver must have been awake, struggling to maintain control. Third, Pipkin noted that the car tracks "arced" to the right just before hitting the wing wall, an indication that the driver not only was awake but was making a conscious effort to get back onto the highway.

Based on these observations, Pipkin hypothesized that

Silkwood's Honda had crossed the road after being banged by another vehicle. Either the percussion itself, or the percussion combined with overreaction by the driver, had forced the car off the road. Would he find any evidence on the car itself that would confirm this hypothesis?

Pipkin jacked the Honda up so he could examine its underbelly. Then he crawled all over the car, measuring and taking pictures. He noted that the sides of the steering wheel were bent forward. When an unconscious body falls against a steering wheel on impact, it bends the *top and bottom* forward, not the sides. That detail confirmed what the tire treads told him—Silkwood was awake, conscious, and gripping the wheel. She had locked her elbows against the crash.

Next, Pipkin noted that the rear bumper was covered with a film of road dust except for a two-inch dent on the left side. The edge of the left fender next to the dent was also damaged. Horizontal scratches in the dent indicated that they were made by an object moving from rear to front.

Recognizing that Silkwoood's death was a high-profile case, Pipkin hired an engineer and a chemist to supplement his findings. The engineer studied the dent with a high-powered magnifier and concluded that the horizontal direction of the scratches precluded damage caused by scraping or banging when the tow truck pulled the car out of the ditch. If the damage had occurred during extraction, the scratches would have been perpendicular and the dent filled with dirt or concrete dust. The dent would have been rough like sandpaper. Instead, it was smooth, oval, and clean. He concluded that the dent was made by a "glancing" blow that would not have changed the direction or speed of the car but was forceful enough to cause the driver to overreact and lose control.

The findings of the chemist supported the conclusions of the engineer. He found no cement, sand, red clay, mud, or road dirt in the dent. He did find, however, black marks across the top of and inside the dent. The smudges tested positive for rubber.

Three weeks after Silkwood's death, Pipkin submitted his report to Tony Mazzocchi. Appended to the document were the analyses of the consulting engineer and chemist, and twenty photographs. The report concluded that all the evidence Pipkin found, though circumstantial, was interlocking, consistent, and in agreement. It all pointed to one conclusion—Silkwood was forced off the road.

Nevertheless, Rick Fagen stood by his report. The Oklahoma Highway Patrol defended him, maintaining that the dent was made when the wrecker pulled the car from the ditch. Although someone hired the Pinkerton detective agency to dig into Pipkin's background, Pinkerton detectives found nothing to impugn his credibility. The Pinkerton report ended up in the files of Kerr-McGee.

✦

The autopsy report was the final document dealing with the death of Karen Silkwood. The medical examiner's stated cause of death was predictable—multiple fractures, contusions, lacerations, and abrasions. He went on to say that a toxicological analysis showed that Silkwood had .35 mg of methaqualone (the narcotic in Quaaludes) in her blood. A therapeutic dose was .25 mg, he said. A toxic dose was .50 mg. He pointed out that there was a half capsule of Quaalude in Silkwood's stomach, but it was only partially digested. He concluded that Silkwood was under the influence of a sedative-hypnotic drug the night she died, and therefore her death was an accident. Then he drew a conclusion that went well beyond the protocol and mandate of his job. He said that the dent in the bumper of Silkwood's car was made when the Honda was extracted from the ditch. He had not examined the dent.

A Silkwood attorney deposed the medical examiner several years after her death.

How did he know it was a one-car accident, the attorney asked. Because the Oklahoma Highway Patrol said it was, the medical examiner said.

How did he know that the methaqualone in Silkwood's blood actually induced her to fall asleep at the wheel? It was a judgment call made by his toxicologist, the medical examiner answered.

Isn't it possible, if not likely, that Silkwood had built up a tolerance for the drug after using it for three months, the attorney asked? That would be speculation, the medical examiner replied.

✦

Under prodding by Tony Mazzocchi, the Department of Justice reluctantly asked the FBI to open an investigation into the death of Karen Silkwood. Then, without notifying Mazzocchi, the Justice Department ordered the Bureau to conduct only a "preliminary" probe and not to examine "possible suspects or motives." In February 1975, two months after Mazzocchi had pressured Justice to open the investigation, someone attempted to murder him. He was driving back to Washington from the Airlie House conference center fifty miles west of D.C. He had been attending a meeting on worker saftey followed by an informal get-together. Twenty minutes after he left Airlie House, Mazzocchi blacked out at the wheel. His car drifted right, shot over an embankment, missed a group of trees, and landed on its roof. Mazzocchi was tossed from the car. By the time the ambulance arrived, he was alive but hallucinating about World War II. He suffered some facial contusions and brain lacerations, which eventually healed. He was convinced his martini had been spiked.

On May 1, 1975, five and a half months after the FBI had begun its investigation, the Justice Department closed its probe with a five-page Death Fact Memorandum written by a low-ranking attorney in the department.

Like trooper Fagen's accident report, the Death Fact Memorandum was filled with assumptions as well as minor and major errors of fact. It said, for example, that it was "extremely windy" on the evening Silkwood was killed, suggesting that even if a sleepy driver tended to drift right, a strong crosswind would have pulled the car left. It was a valid observation—except that weather bureau reports said only a light wind was blowing that night.

The memorandum failed to address the issue of Silkwood's missing documents. It failed to challenge the autopsy report that .35 mg of methaqualone would be an overdose for Silkwood.

Two-thirds of the Death Fact Memorandum was an attack on A. O. Pipkin. The report dismissed his finding that Silkwood was awake and struggling to maintain control of the car. Why? The Oklahoma Highway Patrol found no such evidence. The memorandum challenged Pipkin's drift-right observation. Why? *Consumer Reports* said that the Honda Civic tended to drift left and to lunge left during acceleration. What about the dent? The memorandum suggested that Drew Stephens may have purposely made it so it would look as though Silkwood had been forced off the road. The memorandum concluded, "On the basis of the facts produced by the above investigation, it was determined that there was no violation of federal criminal law in the death of Ms. Silkwood." Case closed.

There is good reason to believe that the FBI wrote a longer final report on the killing of Karen Silkwood. Echo told Bill Taylor that he had seen such a report, and that it was classified top secret. In response to a 2014 FOIA request, the FBI said that it could not confirm or deny that a final report on the death of Karen Silkwood does or does not exist. If it does exist, however, it would be exempt from release under a provision in the Freedom of Information Act. It was no surprise that the FBI played the same trump card as the Oklahoma State Bureau of Investigation.

✦

It was Bill Taylor who solved the car-crash mystery. Taylor walked the old accident site looking for clues and explanations before the Silkwood trial opened. He concluded that Karen Silkwood had crossed the highway and hit the left shoulder at a forty-five-degree angle just as Fagen and Pipkin believed. But they had not puzzled out at what point on the highway she began to cross to the other side.

Taylor followed the creek back into the fields. He found

a 1974 New Jersey license plate close to the culvert. He had a source check the tag later. The plate was not renewed in 1975 and there was no recording of it ever being issued in the first place. Taylor concluded that the license belonged to a federal agent of some kind. It was standard practice for each state to issue a certain number of tags to agencies like the FBI without keeping a public record of them.

Like Fagen and Pipkin, Taylor noted a dirt oil service road stretching to the pumps on either side. From an oil drilling rig driver he met on the road, Taylor learned that the land around the road belonged to Sherri Ellis's family. A check of the property deeds confirmed what the rig driver told Taylor. A further check showed that a farmhouse and two barns a mile back from Highway 74 also belonged to the Ellis family. Taylor had a hunch.

The farmhouse was locked up and looked as if no one had lived there for a long time. There was a horse in one barn (Taylor later confirmed that it belonged to Karen's roommate, Sherri Ellis). The other barn was a tractor shed. It was empty. But in the west corner, Taylor found a shelf on which old bottles and junk had been pushed aside, as if to make room for something. He poked around carefully. At the back of the shelf was a brown manila envelope covered with dust and pigeon droppings. On the floor lay a soiled white number ten business envelope. Both envelopes were empty and unaddressed. But both carried the Kerr-McGee logo in the upper-right-hand corner.

Karen must have stashed her documents in the barn, Taylor reasoned. She knew that Sherri kept her horse there, and she had probably visited the farm with her roommate, possibly to go riding. Just a mile from the Cimarron plant, the abandoned shed was an ideal hideout. The farmhouse was empty; she could have come and gone unnoticed. And she could easily drive there after work if she had something to hide.

Taylor speculated that either the barn had been Karen's permanent hiding place for the documents, or that she had kept the evidence in her apartment and then, when the apartment was quarantined because of radiation contamination the week before she died, she had taken the documents to the barn. Taylor admired her strategy. She was too smart to carry sensitive evidence around in her car. After the union meeting at the Hub, she had stopped off at the farm to get the rest of her documents before heading to the Holiday Inn in Oklahoma City. There was no other logical explanation.

Taylor thought the black skid marks on Highway 74 noted by Fagen at the entrance to and exit from the dirt oil road were Silkwood's. The chase car had bumped her, causing her to momentarily lose control of her Honda, fishtail down the highway, then cross to the other side of the road at a forty-five-degree angle, leaving no other skid marks.

Echo confirmed most of Taylor's theory. He told Taylor that he had risked a quick peek into the Bureau's top-secret files called "June Mail," which were kept in a highly secured room, where he found the final report on Silkwood's death. He had time only to read about two-thirds of page 3. To Taylor, Echo sounded scared.

According to the FBI summary report on that page, a car followed Karen Silkwood from the Hub Café, but lost her when she turned west (right), approximately two hundred yards from the death scene, down the narrow oil road. The chase car eventually turned down the same road, looking for Silkwood. It met her returning to Highway 74. The chase car tried to stop her on the oil road, but she sped around it. Then the chase car raced to a turnaround on the right and followed her.

When she reached Highway 74, Silkwood hit her brakes. The chase car slid into the Honda, bumping it.

Silkwood turned left as if to head back to the Hub Café, then swung right toward Oklahoma City, racing onto the grassy left shoulder.

Based on A. O. Pipkin's accident report, Echo's phone call to Bill Taylor, and Taylor's observations, the last moments of Karen Silkwood's life are as clear as they are tragic. When the chase car bumped her Honda, Silkwood overreacted and momentarily lost control. Her car crossed over the highway and hit the grassy shoulder at a forty-five-degree angle. She managed to straighten the car out, and it sped down the bumpy shoulder at approximately fifty miles per hour. As soon as Silkwood regained control, she looked behind her to see how close the chase car was. Then she started to ease the car off the shoulder and back onto the highway. She didn't see the concrete wing wall of the culvert that ran under the road, and her car began to sail through the air. She pushed against the steering wheel to brace herself for collision. The car smashed head-on into the wall. She died instantly.

16

WAS IT WORTH IT?

Snowden

Edward Snowden must be very pleased. He said: "I want to spark a worldwide debate about privacy, Internet freedom, and the dangers of state surveillance. . . . I will be satisfied if the federation of secret law, unequal pardon, and irresistible executive powers that rule the world I love are revealed for even a second."

Assuming Snowden meant what he said, his whistleblowing was a huge success. He did indeed spark a worldwide debate that will continue into the near future as lawmakers, executive leaders, politicians, bureaucrats, and intelligence gatherers condemn and defend the massive invasion of the privacy of suspicionless private citizens. The debate over how to balance freedom and security promises to be long and bitter.

The leak sparked another quiet, unemotional, and reasoned debate among communication companies and law enforcement and intelligence-gathering agencies. The outcome of that debate could radically change how Americans communicate with each other. The debate question is:

should communication companies, device manufacturers, and Internet providers automatically install "ubiquitous encryption" software programs, like the PGP software Edward Snowden uses?

Ubiquitous encryption is end-to-end privacy protection. Only the sender and the recipient hold the encryption key. Ubiquitous encryption would have important and severe security implications that focus, once again, on the privacy versus security debate. The encryption would block law enforcement and intelligence officers from bulk-collecting the private telephone and e-mail messages of Americans. It would also mean that even if the NSA, CIA, or FBI had a legal warrant to tap a private communication, it couldn't. Thus, ubiquitous encryption would be a gift to criminals and terrorists alike.

If the United States adopts ubiquitous encryption, law enforcement and intelligence organizations would like to have either a duplicate encryption key or access to a "back door" built into the device, which would allow them to retrieve coded data and messages. Three former, high-level government officials—Mike McConnell (former NSA director), Michael Chertoff (former Homeland Security director), and William Lynn (former deputy defense director)—have argued in favor of unconditional, ubiquitous encryption in a jointly written article published in the *Washington Post*.

"If law enforcement and intelligence organizations face a future without assured access to encrypted communications," they wrote, "they will develop technologies and techniques to meet their legitimate mission goals."

✦

Opinion polls published since Edward Snowden blew the whistle in June 2013 have not provided much direction in puzzling out what Americans think and feel about Edward Snowden. Those polls have been irregular and spotty, and have failed to follow up longitudinally. More important, each one has asked different questions, making a general assessment of American public opinion little more than an educated guess. The questions various opinion polls have asked include: Do you think Edward Snowden was right or wrong to blow the whistle? Do you think Edward Snowden served the public interest or harmed national security? Do you think Edward Snowden's leaks were helpful or harmful? Do you think the United States should prosecute Edward Snowden? Do you think Edward Snowden is a hero or a traitor?

It's hard to conclude much from comparing apples to oranges.

A KRC poll commissioned by the ACLU (which legally represents Snowden) and published in *U.S. News & World Report*, tried to make sense of public opinion. The survey was both creatively different in scope and surprising in its findings. KRC reported in February 2015 that one-third of Americans had either never heard of Edward Snowden, or had heard his name but knew next to nothing about him. Two-thirds of Americans had heard about Snowden and had seen "at least a small amount of information about him." Of that group, 64 percent had a *negative opinion* of Snowden. It's hard to place a value on that negative number.

In June 2013, two weeks after Snowden blew the whistle, a PEW Research Center survey had reported that a majority of Americans (56 percent) didn't object to NSA's tracking of their phone records to find terrorists. Does the

2015 KRC poll suggest that Snowden had lost support in the United States over the preceding two years? Or were the polling questions so different that a valid comparison is not possible?

KRC went on to poll NSA's snoop partners—Australia, Canada, Great Britain and New Zealand. Unlike Americans, the majority of the citizens polled in those countries held *favorable opinions* about Snowden—Australia (64%), Canada (58%), Great Britain (54%), and New Zealand (51%).

KRC also polled five Western European countries that were NSA targets. The results tell a different story. Among Germans and Italians, 84 percent viewed Edward Snowden *positively*, and about 80 percent of French, Spanish, and Dutch citizens held *favorable opinions* of Snowden.

How does Snowden himself feel about the less than generous support of his fellow Americans and his unpredictable future? "I have no regrets," he said. "This country is worth dying for."

✦

Great Britain was the first to step up to the plate. In February 2014, nine months after Snowden blew the whistle, the court that oversees British intelligence and security agencies ruled that GCHQ, Britain's electronic spy agency, had acted unlawfully when it received intercepted communications from NSA's top-secret PRISM program. The court—the Investigatory Powers Tribunal—ruled that when GCHQ failed to make its snooping deal with the NSA public, it breached the human rights of British citizens and violated the provisions of the European Convention on Human Rights. It was the first time the court had ever ruled against any of Britain's intelligence agencies.

That ruling doesn't mean that GCHQ will stop bulk, warrantless data mining. It may very well rename the operation and continue snooping on British citizens. Or it may create new, legally suspect intelligence operations in accordance with its stated goal, which was to master the Internet. However GCHQ responds, it is unlikely it has abandoned that mission.

It took U.S. courts a little longer to reach the same conclusion about the bulk harvesting of phone data on Americans. In May 2015, two years after Snowden blew the whistle, the U.S. Second Circuit Court of Appeals ruled that bulk collection and storage of phone data was illegal. In effect, the court ruled that NSA bulk collection programs were not only a distortion of the USA PATRIOT Act, but a violation of both the First and Fourth Amendments, making them unconstitutional.

The suit against the government was filed by the ACLU. Its attorneys argued that dragnet collection "gives the government a comprehensive record of our associations and public movements, revealing a wealth of detail about our familial, political, professional, and religious associations. [It] is likely to have a chilling effect on whistleblowers and others." The lower court ruled in favor of the government. The three-judge appeals court panel unanimously overturned that decision.

The appeals court's ninety-seven-page opinion pulled no punches. It called the bulk collection of phone data "staggering . . . [an] unprecedented contraction of the privacy expectation of all Americans." The court went on to reject

NSA's plan to stockpile information that might be relevant in the future. "Such an expansive concept of 'relevance' is unprecedented and unwarranted," the court ruled. "At its core, the approach boils down to the proposition that essentially all the telephone records were relevant to essentially all international terrorism investigations."

Since the Patriot Act is a congressional act, the appeals court left it up to Congress to either repeal it or modify it to make it constitutional. In June 2015, Congress allowed the Patriot Act to expire, making bulk collection of phone records illegal. Then it passed a compromise law, the USA Freedom Act, which follows the lead of the appeals court and condemns the bulk collection and storage of Americans' phone data but keeps the door open to harvesting the phone records of suspected terrorists. It also narrows the collecting of other types of records such as e-mails. And it increases the transparency of the surveillance court's top-secret decisions.

We should not be surprised if the privacy-versus-intelligence-collection issue eventually lands in the lap of the U.S. Supreme Court in the not-too-distant future. Equally, we should not be surprised if the NSA, which lies to Congress to cover its tracks, creates new massive intelligence-gathering programs with deceptive code names to circumvent the Freedom Act. If the NSA chooses to once again challenge or violate the First and Fourth Amendments, it just might create another Edward Snowden.

✦

Edward Snowden was worried that Americans would yawn at the revelations of the government's massive and unconstitutional invasion of their privacy. "I have only one fear doing all of this," he said, "which is that people will see these documents and shrug, that they'll say, 'We assumed this is happening and don't care.' The only thing I'm worried about is that I'll do all this to my life for nothing."

If one had to select a single word to describe the attitude of the majority of Americans about Snowden's revelations, it would be *apathy*. Unlike the majority of British citizens, who were outraged and vocal about the invasion of their privacy, the majority of Americans have remained silent and defeated. A Pew Research Center survey taken right after the first Snowden leaks found that a majority of Americans (56 percent) did not object to NSA's tracking of their phone records to find terrorists. A 2015 Pew Research study reported that 93 percent of adults in the study said that being in control of who can get information about them is very important. But most of them aren't using digital tools that could protect their privacy.

It turns out that, for most people, privacy is an important abstract issue that does not excite them, rather than a visceral one that would. Government invasion of privacy in the abstract does not touch the pocketbook or capture the imagination. It is not a life-or-death issue, the fear of terrorists notwithstanding. Although public opinion is as fickle as the weather, it is unlikely that most Americans will ever get wrought up over warrantless and illegal telephone data harvesting. As the *Christian Science Monitor* put it: "In recent years . . . the public has mostly yawned over the need for a privacy-data discussion. The zeitgeist had evolved to a point where most people know that their daily activities leave countless digital traces. Data collection is like the rain, it will be there, whether we like it or not. This seems especially true when it comes to fighting terrorism."

Edward Snowden asks a final, Thoreau-like question that challenges such apathy: If a society cedes its privacy to the government and its secret intelligence agencies, is that society really free?

17

WAS IT WORTH IT?

Silkwood

At first glance, it looks as if Karen Silkwood died for nothing. The only ones who seemingly benefited from her death were her enemies. A deeper examination, however, reveals that Silkwood made a difference in ways she could not have foreseen.

Karen Silkwood meticulously collected health, safety, and quality-control documents—undercover and quietly—for two months. She wanted to expose conditions at the Kerr-McGee Cimarron plant and embarrass the company into making health and safety concessions during contract negotiations. Her documents never got to the *New York Times*. There was no exposé. The union failed to win a single health and safety concession from Kerr-McGee. And the corporation was not fined for the health and safety violations that Silkwood had exposed to the AEC in Bethesda, Maryland, less than two months before she was killed.

Although the Cimarron plant closed a few months after her death, the shutdown had nothing to do with Karen

Silkwood. Kerr-McGee had filled the AEC's order for fuel rods and the plant was no longer needed. Today, the contaminated facility sits on a bluff overlooking the Cimarron River, secured and abandoned. No one seems to know how badly it polluted the river and the underground aquifers the river feeds.

Two months after Silkwood's death, the U.S. Congress replaced the AEC with the Energy Research and Development Administration (ERDA) and the Nuclear Regulatory Commission (NRC). The plan to reshape how the government promotes and regulates the nuclear industry had been on the drafting board months before Silkwood blew the whistle at AEC headquarters.

After the death of his daughter, Bill Silkwood devoted the remainder of his life to finding out who killed her and why. He filed a civil suit in a federal court alleging that named individuals at Kerr-McGee and a list of law enforcement and intelligence agencies deprived his daughter of her civil rights through wiretapping, bugging, and illegal surveillance, then conspired to cover it up.

Federal judge Luther Bohannon threw a wrench in Bill Silkwood's argument. Appointed to the bench through the intervention of Senator Robert Kerr (cofounder of Kerr-McGee), Bohannon thought that the conspiracy allegation against a bevy of upstanding citizens and community leaders was preposterous and unfounded. Furthermore, he found that the Silkwood legal team had little or no concrete evidence to prove their wiretapping conspiracy case. He refused to grant motions to subpoena alleged conspirators, calling them a fishing expedition. And he refused to extend the discovery period, killing the legal case and forcing the Silkwood team to narrow its focus. It now argued that Kerr-McGee had deprived Karen Silkwood of her civil rights as a union official. The legal theory was based on the Civil Rights Act of 1871.

Bohannon's successor, Judge Frank G. Theis, didn't buy the application of the Civil Rights Act to Karen Silkwood. He ruled that the law was originally passed to provide black persons, terrorized by such groups as the Ku Klux Klan, the means to get equal protection under the law. Karen Silkwood was not black. Therefore, there was no legal racial bias in the Silkwood case. An appeals court would later uphold Theis's decision.

The Silkwood legal team narrowed its case yet again. It now charged Kerr-McGee with gross negligence in safeguarding the plutonium that contaminated Karen Silkwood in her apartment a week before she was killed. In effect, the back-to-back legal decisions had precluded introducing any evidence dealing with wiretapping, harassment, and wrongful death, including murder or manslaughter.

But in 1979, almost five years after Karen Silkwood's death, the Silkwood family won a major victory. An Oklahoma jury found Kerr-McGee guilty of gross negligence and awarded them $10.5 million (about $30 million today) for physical and emotional pain, bodily injury, and punitive damages. By 1970 standards, the amount was huge, if not precedent setting.

Bill Silkwood was of course pleased with the national publicity, the verdict, and the award. He was especially happy that the jury ruled that his daughter did not contaminate herself. Silkwood friends called the verdict a vindication of her work as a whistleblower and a reclamation of her name and reputation. The world now knew that Karen Gay Silkwood had been right about the life-threatening health and safety conditions at Kerr-McGee's Cimarron plant.

Kerr-McGee appealed. Without admitting guilt, it argued that $10.5 million in personal and punitive damages was excessive and it asked the court to reduce the amount. The appeals court dodged the bullet by ordering a new trial. In order to avoid another expensive and image-bashing display, Kerr-McGee made Bill Silkwood an offer—$1.38 million, with no admission of guilt.

Bill Silkwood, who was ill at the time and didn't have the stamina or funds to go through another lengthy trial, accepted the offer. He would spend his remaining years—and his share of the settlement money—trying to chase down his daughter's killers. He hired investigators—and even psychics—to no avail. The trail was cold, doors were locked, and lips were sealed. Bill Silkwood died without answers.

The futility of Bill Silkwood's private investigation into his daughter's death is not surprising. It was doomed from the start. Soon after Judge Theis announced a trial date, Echo called Bill Taylor. As part of its pretrial discovery, the Silkwood legal team had subpoenaed all the FBI files dealing with Karen Silkwood. The Bureau released approximately two thousand pages filled with as many holes as a kitchen sieve. Echo told Taylor that the files were filled with top-secret documents dealing with the wiretapping and surveillance of Karen Silkwood.

"The Bureau hasn't given you 60 percent of the Silkwood file," Echo said. "You'd need a truck to cart the boxes around. Thousands and thousands of papers. The damn case has files from here to Union Station."

Echo also told Taylor, "The Silkwood case is a doozie. The Bureau is covering so much shit on Silkwood, you wouldn't believe me."

"Try me," Taylor said. "Was she murdered?"

"I don't know," Echo said. "Everyone is tight-lipped. A lot of agents have been called on the carpet. One [of them] threatened the Bureau. 'If I'm marked,' he said 'I'll tell all.'"

That agent was most likely Larry Olson, who directed the Silkwood investigation in Oklahoma.

Olson confirmed Echo's allegation that the FBI had smothered the Silkwood case. Olson told congressional investigator Peter Stockton that the case "was buried so deep you will never get to the bottom of it." Olson ought to know. He directed the FBI investigation of the contamination and death of Karen Silkwood from the Bureau's Oklahoma City office.

But Karen Silkwood would be pleased to know is that, in the light of history, she didn't die in vain. Her life and death had a positive impact on future whistleblowers through an amendment to the Energy Reorganization Act of 1974. As one expert on whistleblowing put it, "Her case triggered a series of nuclear safety exposés, which led Congress to pass nuclear whistleblower protections."

✦

What about Kerr-McGee? Like a cat with nine lives, the corporation managed to land on its feet. According to the Justice Department, the corporation left a trail of more than 250 abandoned and contaminated sites across the country, stretching from Connecticut to California. When Kerr-

McGee learned that the Environmental Protection Agency (EPA) was about to make it pay for the cleanup of those sites, its corporate officers hid the company's liabilities, then sold the company to Anadarko, a major oil conglomerate, for an impressive profit. The sale forced the EPA to sue Kerr-McGee's new owner, Anadarko.

In 2014, the U.S. Department of Justice represented the EPA and more than ten state environmental agencies in a class-action suit against Anadarko. The Justice Department estimated that it would cost nearly $20 billion to decontaminate Kerr-McGee's toxic, abandoned sites. The court awarded the plaintiffs only $5.2 billion. American taxpayers will have to pay the remaining estimated $15 billion or live with the contaminated sites and their health hazards.

AFTERWORD

The Snowden case is far from over. It lacks the perspective only time can give. And the future of Edward Snowden dangles in the breeze of uncertainty.

Where will he go if Russia decides to expel him?

Will he agree to return to the United States to stand trial?

If so, will he be convicted and sentenced to jail?

Will he be assassinated?

The Snowden case has also bequeathed a broader, more critical question for time to answer: Did Snowden do more harm than good? He exposed illegal and unconstitutional intelligence-gathering programs. Those programs will be abandoned by law, a decisive victory for the privacy of all Americans. On the other hand, did Snowden irreparably damage the security of America? And there's the rub. There are so many distortions and lies about the serious impact the Snowden leaks are having on intelligence gathering and the safety of intelligence officers that the public doesn't know who or what to believe. The catch–22 argument they face goes like this: The intelligence community can prove that Snowden endangered the security of Americans and the lives of intelligence agents, but you'll have to take their word for it. The proof is classified.

Ironically, the critical issue of whether Snowden has done more harm than good is shrouded in layers of secrecy and posturing. Perhaps the only one who might shed some light on it would be another Edward Snowden. If one eventually dares to step forward and blow the whistle, it's likely that only historians will be interested in the answer.

✦

Like Edward Snowden, Karen Silkwood leaves a trail of questions. The answers are buried in the file cabinets and vaults of a federal court, the Oklahoma Bureau of Investigation, and the Federal Bureau of Investigation. Ironically, the top-secret information is protected from disclosure and lawsuits by a clause in the Freedom of Information Act. Professionals involved in FOIA litigation are especially frustrated because that clause exempts seven categories of "records and information compiled for law enforcement purposes." FOIA litigators believe that the loophole should be revisited and revised. If it isn't, the warning that FBI agent Lawrence Olson issued to a congressional investigator nearly forty years ago will remain true: The Silkwood case is "buried so deep you will never get to the bottom of it."

Unless a whistleblower leaks secret files to the media.

But the Karen Silkwood case offers something that Edward Snowden's cannot—forty years of distance in grappling with the question: Was more harm done that than good? History tells us that Silkwood did no harm to her fellow workers, the environment, the Cold War, and her fellow Americans. On the contrary, history tells us she did much good. She blew the whistle on the corruption, rot, greed, deception, and disregard of human life rampant in the nuclear industry and at the Atomic Energy Commission. She influenced the passage of health and safety provisions to protect nuclear workers and the environment. She influenced the lawmakers who passed legislation to protect the whistleblowers who followed her. She inspired millions of women.

And still does.

MAJOR SOURCES
AND NOTES

MAJOR SOURCES

Snowden

Greenwald, Glenn. *No Place to Hide*. New York: Henry Holt, 2014. Greenwald is the most important player in the Snowden drama. The first half of his book outlines how he came to meet and interview Snowden in Hong Kong and how he wrote or co-wrote the first series of articles based on the Snowden leaks. His eyewitness account is filled with quotations from Snowden and I rely on him as a primary source, second only to Snowden himself. If there are two or more versions of an event, I generally accept Greenwald. The second half of *No Place to Hide* is a series of documents from the Snowden files.

Harding, Luke. *The Snowden Files*. New York: Vintage Books, 2014. Harding is a reporter for the *Guardian* newspaper, a major player in the Snowden drama. His work is valuable because he has firsthand knowledge about the paper's decision-making process. His colleague Ewan MacAskill is the *Guardian* reporter who authored or coauthored many of the articles based on the Snowden leaks. Harding is also an important source for a description and analysis of the British intelligence agency GCHQ and an excellent source for the reaction of the British public and the British government to the Snowden leaks.

Gurnow, Michael. *The Edward Snowden Affair: Exposing the Politics and Media Behind the NSA Scandal*. Indianapolis: Blue River Press, 2014. Gurnow's book is a well-documented, fresh, and insightful analysis of the Snowden case from several perspectives. He deals in depth with issues that Harding and Greenwald do not address and has added background and facts about Snowden that are not found in Greenwald and Harding.

Andrews, Suzanna, Bryan Burrough, and Sarah Ellison. "The Snowden Saga: A Shadowland of Secrets and Light." *Vanity Fair,* May 2014. This magazine article is useful from the human interest point of view, offering details about Snowden's personal life and observations that both characterize and humanize him.

The Guardian, 2013–2015. The newspaper is an ongoing, reliable, and invaluable source. Not only does it reveal the content of the Snowden leaks, it provides dozens of interviews with Snowden, online chats, background stories, and public and government reactions to the leaks. It also gives voice to Snowden's critics.

Christian Science Monitor, New York Times, Washington Post, 2013–2015. These newspapers provided important background stories, reaction stories, and critical analysis.

Although I rely on the sources listed above for information, the organization of that information and the analysis of the data are totally mine unless otherwise indicated.

Silkwood

Rashke, Richard. *The Killing of Karen Silkwood.* Boston: Houghton Mifflin, 1981. Most of the Silkwood facts are based on my book, which is heavily documented. New facts, new background sources, and interviews are duly noted in the chapter notes below. Quotes taken from the book are referenced by page number. Because more than forty years have passed since Silkwood's death, a reanalysis of her story was needed in the light of history. In particular, the role that the Atomic Energy Commission played in her brief life is new and more incisive than it could have been in 1981. Finally, some of the information, observations, and conclusions presented in the Silkwood story are based on documents recently declassified under a Freedom of Information request.

I have also used the following two books as information sources:

Kohn, Howard. *Who Killed Karen Silkwood?* New York: Summit, 1981. Kohn's book, published just after mine, furnishes valuable information about the early life of Silkwood, her relationship with her boyfriend Drew Stephens, her union contact Steve Wodka, and other movers and shakers in the Silkwood story.

Srouji, Jacque. *Critical Mass.* Nashville: Aurora, 1977. Srouji's book also contains some fresh information about Silkwood's early life. Her appendix contains several useful documents.

Whistleblowing

Elliston, Frederick, John Keenan, Paula Lockhart, and Jan van Schaick. *Whistleblowing Research: Methodical and Moral Issues*. New York: Praeger, 1985.

Glazer, Myron, and Penina Glazer. *The Whistleblowers: Exposing Corruption in Government and Industry*. New York: Basic Books, 1989.

Kohn, Stephen Martin. *The Whistleblower's Handbook: A Step-by-Step Guide to Doing What's Right and Protecting Yourself*. Guilford, CT: Lyons Press, 2011.

Miethe, Terance D. *Whistleblowing at Work: Tough Choices in Exposing Fraud, Waste, and Abuse on the Job*. Boulder, CO: Westview Press, 1999.

Rost, Peter, MD. *The Whistleblower: Confessions of a Healthcare Hitman*. Brooklyn, NY: Soft Skull Press, 2006.

Rothschild, Joyce. "Freedom of Speech Denied, Dignity Assaulted: What Whistleblowers Experience in the U.S." Typescript, courtesy of the author.

————. "Rising in Defense of Non-profit Organizations' Social Purposes: How do whistleblowers fare when they expose corruption in non-profits?" Paper submitted to the Special Symposium on Values, Culture and Democracy in Non-profits, NVSQ, 2012. Typescript, courtesy of the author.

Rothschild, Joyce, and Terance D. Miethe. "Whistle-Blower Disclosures and Management Retaliation: The Battle to Control Information about Organization Corruption. *Work and Occupations,* February 1999.

Soeken, Donald. *Don't Kill the Messenger: How America's Valiant Whistleblowers Risk Everything in Order to Speak Out Against Waste, Fraud and Abuse in Business and Government*. North Charleston, SC: CreateSpace Independent Publishing Platform, 2014.

Soeken, Donald and Karen Soeken. "A Survey of Whistleblowers: Their Stressor and Coping Strategies." Laurel, MD: Integrity International, undated.

Vinton, Gerald, ed. *Whistleblowing: Subversion or Corporate Citizenship?* New York: St. Martin's Press, 1994.

NOTES

1. The Whistleblower's Dilemma

9 *Remain silent,* Rothschild, "Freedom of Speech Denied," 13. This paper is a summary of the survey findings conducted by Rothschild and Miethe.

9 *Were naïve,* Rothschild and Miethe, 119.

9 *Reported the wrongdoing internally,* Ibid., 112.

9 "Personally held values," Ibid., 119.

9 *Forced to resign,* Rothschild, "Rising in Defense," 10.

9 *Shunned,* Ibid., 10.

9 *Severe depression; decline in physical health; severe financial decline; family relations,* Ibid., 10-11.

9 "Systemic," Rothschild and Miethe, 125.

10 "Up to five years," Soeken and Soeken, 9.

10 *No significant positive change,* Rothschild, "Rising in Defense of Non-Profits," 13.

10 *Wrongdoer unpunished,* Ibid., 18.

2. Disillusioned: Edward Snowden

11 *Called him a genius,* Suzanna Andrews, Bryan Burrough, and Sarah Ellison.

11 *High-level government officials,* Greenwald develops his argument in *With Liberty and Justice for Some.* New York: Henry Holt, 1981.

12 "By ordering," Greenwald, *No Place to Hide,* 2.

12 "Snowden was highly," Ibid, 40.

13 *Barely remember him,* Carol D. Leonnig, Jena Johnson and Marc Fisher, "Leaker of Secrets Preferred to Keep his Own Life Hidden," *Washington Post,* June 16, 2013. Also Gurnow, 2.

13 "The protagonist," *No Place to Hide,* 46.

14 *Mononucleosis,* Gurnow, 2.

14 "I don't even have," Ibid.

14 *IQ was 140,* Ibid., 11.

14 *Claiming to be a moderate,* Suzanna Andrews, Bryan Burrough, and Sarah Ellison.

14 "Loved to death," Harding, 17.

15 "Who the fuck are," *Guardian,* February 1, 2014. The article is a long critique and summary of Harding's book, which analyzes Snowden's blog postings.

15 *Silly photos,* Ibid.

15 "So Sexy." Both Harding and Gurnow quote extensively from Snowden's Ars Technica blogs.

16 "I wanted to fight," Harding, 22.

16 "Fighting soldiers from the sky." Lyrics are from "Ballad of the Green Berets," by Robert Moore and Staff Sgt. Barry Sadler, published in 1966.

16 "My visual acuity," Harding, 24.

17 *Broke both legs,* Spencer Ackerman, "Special Forces: Whistleblower Did Try to Enlist," *Guardian,* June 11, 2013.

17 "Most of the people," Harding, 23.

18 *One in four,* Robert O'Harrow, Dana Priest, and Marjorie Censer, "Amid Rise of Outsourcing, Shakier Vetting," *Washington Post,* June 11, 2013.

19 "It was tough," Harding, 24; *Guardian,* February 1, 2014; and Suzanna Andrews, Bryan Burrough, and Sarah Ellison.

19 The description of what Snowden did in Geneva is based mostly on the *Guardian*, February 1, 2014.

19 "Cyber cop," Harding, 44.

20 "Crisis of conscience," Harding, 35; and *Guardian*, February 1, 2014.

20 "Much of what I saw," Gurnow, 10.

20 "When you leak," *No Place to Hide*, 43.

21 "I could watch drones," Ibid.

22 Kunia description is based on Harding, 41–42.

22 Lindsay Mills. See: Harding, Ibid.; Tom Leonard, "The Pole Dancer Left Behind," *Daily Mail* (London), June 12, 2013; Paul Lewis, "Whistleblower's Girlfriend," *Guardian*, June 12, 2013; Raf Sanchez and Nick Allen, "The Pole-Dancer and Her Man of Mystery," *The Daily Telegraph*, June 12, 2013.

22 "A world where," Harding, 48.

23 *Booz Allen Hamilton*, Neil Irwin, "7 Facts about Booz Allen Hamilton," *Washington Post*, June 11, 2013; and Catherine Rampell, "Booz Allen Reaps Big Profits From U.S.," *New York Times*, June 11, 2013.

23 *Whistleblower-in-waiting*, *Guardian*, February 1, 2014.

24 "I realized they were building," *No Place to Hide*, 47–48.

24 "[Obama] closed the door," Gurnow, 19.

25 *Epilepsy, No Place to Hide*, 48.

3. Disillusioned: Karen Silkwood

27 Bill Silkwood's background comes from his detailed obituary, a hand-written copy of which was provided to the author by Karen Silkwood's son, Michael Meadows.

27 Details of Silkwood's early life come from Kohn, Rashke, and Srouji.

30 *"Classified specifications."* The question of whether the AEC/Kerr-McGee documents in Kerr-McGee's files were classified is bureaucratic. The documents in AEC files dealing with plutonium, plutonium management, and fuel rod production are classified. It's not clear whether those same documents stored in Kerr-McGee files are marked "classified." If not, it's not clear whether they legally could be called "classified."

4. Whom to Tell: Snowden

35 "Those efforts," *No Place to Hide*, 42.

35 *Four superiors*, Ellen Nakashima and Barton Gellman, "U.S., Snowden Duel Over E-mails," *Washington Post*, May 30, 2014.

36 *Seventy-two hours*, Suzanna Andrews, Bryan Burrough, and Sarah Ellison.

37 "Livid that the," *No Place to Hide*, 18.

37 "All the worst," Ibid., 54.

37 "To control disclosures," Ibid., 55.

37 "All the ways," Ibid.

37 "The *Post* editorial page," Ibid., 54.

37 *Blocked the publication,* Ibid., 55.

38 "The security of people's," Ibid., 7.

39 "Here I am ready," Ibid., 10.

39 "Blowing off one," Ibid.

39 *Poitras watch list,* Suzanna Andrews, Bryan Burrough, and Sarah Ellison.

39 "A notable thorn," Harding, 7.

40 "I am a senior member." The story and quotations about Poitras's first contact with Snowden are from the *Guardian*, February 1, 2014.

40 "I don't know if" and other reaction quotes are from Suzanna Andrews, Bryan Burrough, and Sarah Ellison.

42 "One of the most focused," *No Place to Hide*, 11.

42 "Honest and serious," Ibid., 12.

43 "I have been working with," Ibid., 16. Also following e-mail quotes.

43 "Bizarre." Greenwald discusses his reaction to Hong Kong. Ibid., 16-17.

44 "A spirited commitment," Glenn Greenwald, Ewan MacAskill, and Laura Poitras, *Guardian*, June 10, 2013.

44 *Human Rights Watch,* Paul Owen, "Edward Snowden Not Safe in Hong Kong Warns Human Rights Leader," *Guardian*, June 11, 2013.

45 "Just a very small taste," *No Place to Hide*, 20.

45 "Brassbanner," Barton Gellman, "I did it for Freedom," Cape Argus (South Africa), June 12, 2013.

45 "It was unbelievable," *No Place to Hide*, 20.

46 "Had a longstanding," Christine Haughney and Noam Cohen, "Guardian Makes Waves, and is Ready for More," *Guardian*, June 11, 2013.

46 "I have a huge story," Ibid., 21.

47 "The Guinness is good," Suzanna Andrews, Bryan Burrough, and Sarah Ellison.

47 *Was happy with, No Place to Hide*, 26-30. Story and quotes.

47 "A pretty senior bureaucrat," *Guardian*, February 1, 2014.

48 "folders and then," *No Place to Hide*, 20.

48 The meeting in the Mira Hotel and quotes are based on *No Place to Hide*, 33ff.; Harding, 6-9; and *Guardian*, February 1, 2014.

48 "I had expected," *Guardian*, February 1, 2014.

49 "Sorry," *No Place to Hide*, 37.

49 "He radiated a sense of," Harding, 13.

50 "There are all sorts of documents," Greenwald, MacAskill, and Poitras, "I Have No Intentions of Hiding," *Guardian*, June 10, 2013.

5. Whom To Tell: Silkwood

52 "Surprise," Silkwood trial testimony of Kenneth Plowman. Rashke, 337.

56 *Thirty-nine specific,* Ibid., 22-23.

57 "To allow someone," Silkwood trial testimony of Dr. Karl Z. Morgan, Ibid., 334-335.

58 *Wodka didn't trust,* Ibid., 23-24.

59 *Not tell anyone,* Ibid.

6. Why: Snowden

62 "TOP SECRET" and all other PRISM quotes are from Greenwald, "NSA Collecting Phone Records of Millions of Verizon Customers Daily," *Guardian,* June 6, 2013.

62 FISC, Ibid.

63 The PRISM description is based on Greenwald, *No Place to Hide*; Greenwald and MacAskill, "NSA Prism Program Taps Into User Data of Apple, Google and Others," *Guardian,* June 7, 2013; Barton Gellman, "U.S. Intelligence Mining Data From Nine U.S. Internet Companies in Broad Secret Program," *Washington Post,* June 6, 2013.

64 Description of PRISM slide. Greenwald, *No Place to Hide,* 110. The page features a photograph of the slide.

64 "Information collected under," Nick Hopkins, "UK Gathering Secret Intelligence Via Covert NSA Operation," *Guardian,* June 7, 2013.

65 "You can't have," *Guardian,* "National Court: Surveillance: What they said," June 9, 2013.

65 *Expressed public outrage* (and quotes) are from Dominic Rushe, "Facebook and Google Insisted They Did Not Know of Prism Surveillance Program," *Guardian,* June 8, 2013. Also: Cecilia Kang, "Tech Executives Deny NSA Claims," *Washington Post,* June 8, 2013.

65 "[They] went through several." "Snowden Q and A," *Guardian,* June 18, 2013.

66 BOUNDLESS INFORMANT is based on: *No Place to Hide* and Greenwald and MacAskill, "BOUNDLESS INFORMANT: The NSA's Secret Tool For Tracking Global Surveillance," *Guardian,* June 9, 2013.

67 The GCHQ material is based on: Hopkins, Guardian, June 7, 2013; "Prism: Ministers Challenged over GCHQ's Access to Covert Operations," *Guardian,* June 7, 2013; Peter Beaumont and Toby Helm, "Ministers Forced to Reveal British Link to US Data Spying Scandal," *Guardian,* June 9, 2013; Harding, 155-167; and Gurnow, 75-107.

67 *Fifty-thousand GCHQ files,* Harding, 171.

68 *197 intelligence reports,* Hopkins, *Guardian,* June 7, 2013.

68 *Training courses,* Harding, 163.

68 "As much as 25%," Ibid., 157.

68 *More than two hundred,* Ibid., 164.

69 *Thirty-nine billion events,* Harding, 161.

69 *NSA's 850,* , Gurnow, 98–99.

69 *30, triggers,* Ibid.

69 *Up to thirty days,* Ibid., 97.

69 *More than 175 million pounds,* Harding, 158.

69 *Bugged foreign leaders,* Ibid., 177.

69 *Code names,* Ibid., 171.

70 "My sole purpose," *No Place to Hide,* 23. The quote is part of Snowden's manifesto written for the media.

71 "The NSA has built," Greenwald, *Guardian,* June 9, 2013.

71 "Everybody, everywhere," Harding, 12.

71 "I became aware/I felt it would," *No Place to Hide, 43.*

71 "I have gone to," Ibid., 32.

71 "Every person remembers," Suzanna Andrews, Bryan Burrough, and Sarah Ellison.

71 "Citizenship carries with it," Ibid., 32.

712 "I don't want to destroy," Ibid., 47.

71 "I will be satisfied," Ibid., 84.

72 "I want to spark," Ibid., 18.

72 "I do not want," Harding, 5.

72 "I don't want," *No Place to Hide,* 45.

72 "I know it's," Ibid., 18.

7. Why: Silkwood

74 "We got eighteen." Undated transcript of a Silkwood phone call to Wodka. The transcript is part of the *Silkwood v. Kerr-McGee* court record. Silkwood's roommate Sheri Ellis had a copy of the document. How she got it is not clear. She left the transcript among her papers when she died in 2012. I quote from Ellis's copy.

75 *Fish kill.* Silkwood trial testimony of James V. Smith, Rashke, 336.

75 "Married to cancer." Silkwood trial testimony of Dr. Jon Gofman, Ibid., 329.

76 "I can't believe," Ibid., 27, 77.

76 "Instead of getting." Telephone call transcript.

77 "You don't *know* that," Rashke, 27.

77 "Steve, this shit." Telephone call transcript.

8. The Price: Snowden

79 "The Obama administration," *No Place to Hide*, 50.

79 For Justice Department charges: Peter Finn and Sari Horwitz, "U.S. Files Charges Against Snowden," *Washington Post*, June 22, 2013.

80 The Binney material is based on "Bio: William Binney and J. Kirk Wiebe," The Government Accountability Project (GAP), 2015.

82 "I understand that," *No Place to Hide*, 13 and 18.

83 *Assassination quotes,* "America's Spies Want Edward Snowden Dead," *Buzzfeed*, February 13, 2015.

9. The Price: Silkwood

85 *Background on the AEC,* Alice L. Buch, *A History of the Atomic Energy Commission*. Washington, D.C.: U.S. Department of Energy History Division, August 1982; and Stephanie Cooke, *In Mortal Hands: A Cautionary History of the Nuclear Age*. New York: Bloomsbury, 2009.

87 "Rotten," Cooke, 252.

89 *The LEIU description,* George O'Toole, "America's Secret Police Network," *Penthouse*, December 1976; Frank Donner, *The Age of Surveillance: The Aims and Methods of America's Political Intelligence System*. New York: Alfred A. Knopf, 1980; and Janel Ballaile, "Wide Police Surveillance Abuse Reported by Quakers," *New York Times,* April 17, 1979.

89 "The most common," O'Toole.

90 *Government radiation experiments on unwitting subjects, Human Experiments*: *An Overview on Cold War Era Programs*. Government Accounting Office, GAO/T-NSIAD-94-266, 1994; *Government-Sponsored Testing on Humans*. Hearings Before the Subcommittee on Administrative Law and Governmental Relations, Committee on the Judiciary, House of Representatives, 103rd Congress, Second Session. Washington, D.C.: Government Printing Office, February 3, 1994; Andrew Golisze. *In the Name of Science: A History of Secret Programs, Medical Research and Human Experimentation*. New York: St. Martin's Press, 2003.

93 *Missing plutonium,* Silkwood trial testimony of James V. Smith. Rashke, 337. Trial testimony of James Noel, Ibid., 342.

93 Author's FOIA request to OSBI, March 21, 2014.

93 Release of newly declassified FBI Silkwood documents, July 2014.

10. Silkwood: Death

95 "Company time," Rashke, 28.

96 "Rock pile," Silkwood trial testimony of James V. Smith, Ibid., 233-234.

96 "They pulled them," Ibid., 233.

96 "[He] would come," Ibid.

96 "That place wasn't," Ibid. 232.

97 "Give her a bad time, Ibid., 234.

97 "You have no right," Ibid., 27.

98 "They're still passing," Silkwood/Wodka telephone call transcript.

101 "Congestive heart failure," Rashke, 279.

102 *According to his two daughters,* author's e-mail correspondence with Lynn Bunting: May 5, 2015; May 7, 2015; May 11, 2015; May 29, 2015; May 32, 2015

102 *Sue Bunting,* Ibid.

110 "Unmitigated lie," Rashke, 330.

11. Demonization: Snowden: Publicity Hound, Coward, Liar

112 *The world's most wanted, No Place to Hide,* 88.

112 "I know the government," Greenwald, MacAskill, and Poitras, "I have No Intention of Hiding," *Guardian,* June 10, 2013.

112 "I don't want public," Ibid.

114 "Unfortunately, the mainstream," MacAskill, "Edward Snowden: US Government Has Destroyed Any Chance of a Fair Trial," *Guardian,* June 17, 2013.

115 "I am not here," *Guardian,* June 12, 2013.

116 "Huge chance," *No Place to Hide,* 51.

116 "The disclosure of secret," MacAskill, *Guardian,* June 17, 2013.

116 *Guaranteed his constitutional right,* Ibid.

116 *Plead guilty,* Steve Kenny, "U.S. Willing to Hold Talks if Snowden Pleads Guilty," *New York Times,* January 24, 2014.

117 "I believe I have," *No Place to Hide,* 18.

117 *Orwellian state,* Mark Mazzetti and David E. Sanger, "Top Intelligence Official Assails Snowden and Seeks Return of Documents," *New York Times,* January 30, 2014.

118 *European parliament,* Andrea Peterson, "Snowden Says Repeated Warnings About NSA Went Unheeded," *Washington Post,* March 8, 2014.

118 *NBC Nightly News.* Quoted in Ellen Nakashima and Barton Gellman, "U.S., Snowden Duel Over E-mails," *Washington Post,* May 30, 2014.

118 *Two superiors in NSA's,* Nakashima and Gellman, *Washington Post,* May 30, 2014.

118 "After extensive investigation," Suzanna Andrews, Bryan Burrough, and Sarah Ellison, May 2014.

119 *Ledgett went on to say,* Ibid.

119 "I directly challenge," Ibid.

12. Demonization: Snowden: Spy, Traitor, Criminal

121 "I'm suspicious." Quoted in Tania Branigan, "Edward Snowden 'Not a Chinese spy,'" *Guardian,* June 17, 2013.

122 "This is a predictable smear," Tania Branigan, "Edward Snowden Flatly Denies Chinese Spy Claims," *Guardian,* June 17, 2013.

123 "Living in the loving arms." "House Intelligence Committee Chair Mike Rogers Says He Would Charge 'Traitor' Edward Snowden with Murder," (British) *Daily Mail,* March 23, 2015.

123 "Under the influence," Brian Knowlton, "U.S. Intelligence Officials Believe Snowden is Working with Russians, Lawmaker Says," *New York Times,* March 24, 2014.

123 Karpichkov background, allegations, and quote: Luke Harding, "Confessions of a KGB Spy," *Guardian,* February 22, 2012; and Nigel Nelson, "Snowden Was a Russian Target Seven Years Ago," (Northern Ireland) *The People,* June 8, 2014.

125 *Safe harbor,* Alec Luhn and Mark Tran, "Edward Snowden Given Permission to Stay in Russia for Three More Years," *Guardian,* August 7, 2014.

126 "My government revoked," Katrina vanden Heuvel and Stephen F. Cohen, "Edward Snowden: A 'Nation' Interview," *The Nation,* October 28, 2014.

126 "There has been no public," Knowlton, *New York Times,* March 24, 2014.

126 "No relationship with," Greg Miller, "U.S. Hoped Snowden Would Slip. He Didn't," *Washington Post,* June 15, 2014.

126 "When Snowden says," Knowlton, *New York Times,* March 24, 2014.

126 *Website job,* Lee Ferran, "NSA Leaker Edward Snowden Has New Job in Russia, Lawyer Says," *ABC News,* October 31, 2013.

127 "I'm not some low-level," Christopher Bucktin, "I'm Not a Low-Level Hacker," (Northern Ireland) *Daily Mirror,* May 29, 2014.

128 The "traitor" allegations are based on: John Bolton, "Edward Snowden's Leaks Are a Grave Threat to U.S. National Security, *Guardian,* June 18, 2013; John Carney, "Report Lifts Lid on US Cyberespionage on China," *South China Morning Post,* June 13, 2013; Peter Grier, "NSA Chief: Snooping Helped Thwart Terrorist Attacks in 20 Countries," *Christian Science Monitor,* June 18, 2013, and "Is NSA Exaggerating Surveillance Successes?" June 18, 2013; Barton Gellman, Julie Tate, and Ashkan Soltani, "Caught up in the NSA Net," *Washington Post,* July 6, 2014; Michael Gerson, "Poisoning Patriotism," *Washington Post,* June 14, 2013; Brad Knickerbocker, "Dick Cheney: Edward Snowden a 'Traitor,'" *Christian Science Monitor,* June 16, 2013; Lana Lam, "Edward Snowden: US Government Has Been Hacking Hong Kong and China for Years," *South China Morning Post,* June 13, 2013; Greg Miller, "U.S. Officials Fear Leaker Has More Classified Files," *Washington Post,* June 14, 2013; Warren Murray, "Edward Snowden's NSA Surveillance Strains

China-US Relations," *Guardian,* June 13, 2013; Dan Roberts, "FBI Mueller Says Spy Tactics Could Have Stopped 9/11 Attacks," *Guardian,* June 13, 2013; David E. Sanger, Charlie Savage, and Michael Schmidt, "NSA Chief Says Phone Record Logs Halted Terror Threats," *New York Times,* June 13, 2013; Steven Swinford, "Terrorists are Rubbing Their Hands in Glee," *The Telegraph,* November 7, 2013.

129 "Going to get" and other Mike Rogers's quotes. "House Intelligence Committee Chair Mike Rogers Says He Would Charge 'traitor' Edward Snowden with Murder," *Daily Mail,* March 23, 2015.

129 "Should not be underestimated," Peter Rosher, "Edward Snowden Should be Considered for Amnesty, Says Senior NSA Official," *Washington Post,* December 16, 2013.

129 "Needs to look," Brad Knickerbocker, "Dick Cheney: Edward Snowden is a Traitor," *Christian Science Monitor,* June 16, 2013.

129 "We do not yet know," Bolton, *Guardian,* June 18, 2013.

130 "Being called a traitor," Haroon Siddique, "Edward Snowden's Live Q&A: Eight Things We Learned," *Guardian,* June 18, 2013.

130 "I'm neither a traitor," Lana Lam, "Whistle-blower Edward Snowden Talks to the South China Morning Post," *South China Morning Post,* June 13, 2013.

130 "Collect it all," *No place to Hide,* 95.

131 *Zazi and Headey stories,* Brad Knickerbocker, *Christian Science Monitor,* June 16, 2013, and Ed Pilkington, "NSA Surveillance Played Little Role in Foiling Terror Plots, Experts Say," *Guardian,* June 12, 2013.

132 "That's nonsense," Pilkington, *Guardian,* June 12, 2013.

132 "If we lose our ability," Dan Roberts, "FBI Chief Says Spy Tactics Could Have Been Stopped," *Guardian,* June 13, 2013.

132 "We have not yet," Greg Miller, "U.S. Officials Fear Leaker Has More Classified Files," *Washington Post,* June 14, 2013.

133 "Rubbing their hands with glee," Steven Swinford, "Terrorists are Rubbing Their Hands With Glee" after Snowden leaks, *The Telegraph,* November 7, 2013.

133 "NSA has been," Lana Lam, "Edward Snowden: US Government Has Been Hacking Hong Kong and China for years," *South China Morning Post,* June 13, 2013.

134 *Spying on civilian,* Gurnow, 100-101.

134 Tsinghua University, Ibid, 101.

134 "We hack network," Lam, *South China Morning Post,* June 13, 2013.

134 "What Americans should understand," *Guardian,* June 18, 2013.

135 *MYSTIC,* Ellen Nakashima, "Clapper Bemoans Setback in Spying," *Washington Post,* September 10, 2015.

136 "Meager counterintelligence benefits," Ken Dilanian, "Before Snowden

Leak, NSA Mulled Ending Call Collection," *Washington Post,* March 30, 2015.

136 "I could not do this," Greenwald and MacAskill, "Covert Surveillance: 'We Hack Everyone, Everywhere.'" *Guardian,* June 10, 2013.

137 "We have seen enough," Greenwald, "NSA Whistleblower Edward Snowden: 'I do not Expect to see Home again,'" *Guardian,* June 9, 2013.

137 *Legal discussion,* Julian Borger, "How Edward Snowden Weakened the Case for his Defense," *Guardian,* June 11, 2013; Mark Clayton, "Edward Snowden: Whistleblowing Protections Most likely Won't Help," *Christian Science Monitor,* June 14, 2013; Charlie Savage and Matt Apuzzo, "Snowden Retained Expert in Espionage Defense," *New York Times,* April 29, 2014; Fareed Zakaria, "The People v. Edward Snowden," *Washington Post,* October 24, 2014.

137 "As much as some may want," Borger, *Guardian,* June 11, 2013.

13. A Higher Law?

139 "I cannot in good conscience," *Guardian,* June 11, 2013.

140 *Criteria for civil disobedience,* Elliston, *Whistleblowing Research,* 136.

141 "The government itself," Henry David Thoreau, *On the Duty of Civil Disobedience.* London: The Simple Life Press, 1903, 7.

141 "Must the citizen," Ibid., 9.

141 "Law never made," Ibid.

141 "Most legislators," Ibid., 11.

142 "Unjust laws," Ibid.,18.

142 "It cost me less," Ibid., 26.

142 "[The State] is not," Ibid., 28.

142 "There will never be," Ibid., 33.

142 "The only obligation," Ibid., 9.

14. Demonization: Silkwood

146 *One of eight million,* Harrison, Lana D., Michael Backenheimer, and James A. Inciardi, "Cannabis Use in the U.S.: Implications for a Policy," published in Peter Cohen and Arjan (Eds), *Cannabisheleid in Duitland, Frankriken de Verewigde Staten.* Amsterdam: Centrum voor Drugsonderzoek, University of Amsterdam, 1996.

147 *Enough to buy,* Ibid.

149 "Ask her if she had swallowed," Rashke, 71.

151 *Echo and plutonium,* Ibid. 249-250.

151 For more on diverting uranium and plutonium see: Julian Borger, "The

Truth About Israel's Secret Nuclear Arsenal," *Guardian,* January 15, 2014; Victor Galinsky, "Did Israel Steal Bomb-Grade Uranium from the United States, Report by the Comptroller General, December 18, 1978.

152 *Sticker that said "Kerr-McGee".* The airport account is based on a 1980 interview with Bill Taylor. I decided not to use it in *The Killing of Karen Silkwood.*

153 Jackson report: *U.S. Atomic Energy Commission Division of Inspection, Report 44-2339,* December 19, 1974.

154 "If you can't," Rashke, 74.

156 "There's a lot of," Ibid., 308.

156 "Don't recall saying," Ibid., 309.

15. Asleep at the Wheel? Silkwood

For a complete description of Mazzocchi's accident, see Rashke, 164–165

170 *Summary report, page 3,* Rashke, 380-381.

16. Was It Worth It? Snowden

173 "Want to spark," *No Place to Hide,* 18.

174 *Encryption debate,* Mike McConnell, Michael Chertoff, and William Flynn, "The Key to our Data Future," *Washington Post,* July 31, 2015.

174 "If law enforcement," Ibid.

175 *KRC poll,* Stephen Nelson, *U.S. News,* April 21, 2015.

176 *British Tribunal decision,* Karla Adam, "British Spy Agency Broke law with NSA Data, Tribunal Says," *Washington Post,* February 7, 2014.

177 *U.S. Appeals Court decision,* Ellen Nakashima: "NSA Collection of Phone Data Ruled Unlawful," *Washington Post,* May 8, 2015; "With Deadline Approaching, Lawmakers Introduce Bill to End NSA Program," *Washington Post,* March 29, 2015; "Bulk Records Collection Nearing Endgame," *Washington Post,* May 9, 2015. Also Ellen Nakashima and Mike DeBonis, "White House Pushes for Bill Limiting NSA on Phone Data," *Washington Post,* May 12, 2015. Dan Roberts and Spencer Ackerman, "NSA Phone Surveillance Revealed by Edward Snowden Ruled Illegal," *Guardian,* May 7, 2015.

177 Quotes from the opinion of the U.S. Court of Appeals for the Second Circuit are from Nakashima, *Washington Post,* May 8, 2015; and Roberts and Ackerman, *Guardian,* May 7, 2015.

177 "Gives the government a comprehensive," Charlie Savage, "A.C.L.U. Files Lawsuit Seeking to Stop Collection of Domestic Phone Logs," *New York Times,* June 12, 2013.

179 "I only have one fear," *No Place to Hide,* 19.

179 "In recent years," Cesar Hidalgo, Yves–Alexandre Montjoye, and Alex Pentland, "Solution of NSA Overreach," *Christian Science Monitor,* June 11, 2013.

17. Was It Worth It? Silkwood
185 "Everyone is tight-lipped," Rashke, 197.
185 "Was buried so deep," Rashke, 163.
185 "Her case triggered," Kohn, *Whistleblower's Handbook,* 40.
185 *More than 250 abandoned.* The case was *Tronox Incorporated, et al., (Debtors...Tronox Incorporated Worldwide LLC f/k/a Kerr-McGee Chemical Worldwide LLC, and Tronox LLC f/k/a Kerr-McGee Chemical LLC (plaintiffs) v. Anadarko Petroleum Corporation and Kerr-McGee Corporation (Defendants),* Case No. 09-10156 (ALG), Adv. Pro. 09-1198, March 31, 2010. "Notice of Lodging of Proposed Settlement Agreement Under the federal Debt Collection Procedures Act, Comprehensive Environmental Response, Compensation and Recovery Act, and other Statutes," *The Federal Register,* April 14, 2014; "Case Summary: Tronox Incorporated Bankruptcy Settlement," Environmental Protection Agency, November 23, 2010; Bloomberg, Tiffany Kerry, "Anadarko to dispute $20.8 billion Tronox Claim April 4," *Resource Investor,* March 31, 2014; Ed Crooks, "Anadarko in $5.15bn Pollution Settlement," *Financial Times,* April 4, 2014; Juliet Eilperin, "A Frightening Map of Where Kerr-McGee Polluted, *Washington Post,* April 5, 2014; Juliet Eilperin and Sari Horwitz, "Anadarko to Pay $5.15 Billion to Settle Pollution Case," *Washington Post,* April 4, 2014; Patrick Fitzgerald and Daniel Gilbert, "Anadarko Paying $5 Billion Pollution Dispute," *The Wall Street Journal,* April 4, 2014.